WHEN THE
GOLDEN BOUGH BREAKS

WHEN THE GOLDEN BOUGH BREAKS

Structuralism or Typology?

PETER MUNZ

Professor of History, Victoria University of Wellington, New Zealand

ROUTLEDGE & KEGAN PAUL

LONDON and BOSTON

First published in 1973
by Routledge & Kegan Paul Ltd
Broadway House, 68–74 Carter Lane,
London EC4V 5EL and
9 Park Street
Boston, Mass. 02 108, U.S.A.
Printed in Great Britain by
Willmer Brothers Limited, Birkenhead

ISBN 0 7100 7650 9

To F. L. W. Wood,
in friendship and gratitude

CONTENTS

The impulses which have prompted the writing of this essay on the interpretation of mythology form a set of layers. Peeling them away one by one, there was first a purely intellectual interest in Lévi-Strauss whose system of ideas is the most stimulating challenge of the last two decades. Next came the historian's knowledge that everything has a temporal dimension and that that dimension is of the essence of mythology. The historian need not be concerned much by Lévi-Strauss's comparative lack of interest in the specific historical setting of myths, and indeed might be grateful for his refusal to draw a hard and fast distinction between 'cold' and 'hot' societies. Cold societies are those that seek to annul by special institutions the effects of historical factors on their equilibrium and continuity and hot societies are those that internalise the historical process and make it the moving power of their development. In both cases there is an awareness of history. The distinction between history-conscious and history-unconscious societies is therefore at best a distinction in degree. Myth is produced by primitive peoples and non-primitive peoples alike. The historian can therefore have no *ex officio* quarrel with Lévi-Strauss's comparative lack of interest in historicity as such. But he must be puzzled by his failure to observe the historical seriality of myths and his failure to observe that that seriality is one of their most characteristic properties. There are many things one can consider usefully without paying much attention to their historical dimension. But myth is not one of them. Every myth we know (and the number of myths, though large, is by no means infinite) has both a past and a future. It also occurs both in a more general form and in a more specific form and the historian must equate the more general with the earlier and the more specific with the later form and thus identify the whole phenomenon as a time series. Admittedly, in any one society a myth may occur only in any one form. But since the same or a similar myth also occurs in other societies in more general as well as in more specific forms, the historian is bound to consider this temporal seriality as a phenomenon *sui generis* and take it that any one particular version is a stage in the life-history of the myth. Since he considers these series divorced from the social setting in which they occur, originate and are cultivated, this approach does not commit him to a theory of evolution.

Beyond the historian's concern, there came the philosopher's interest and the attempt to find out the philosophical and, more particularly, the epistemological implications and consequences of the historian's contention that myths present themselves in historical series. It would be idle to pretend that the impulse to work out the philosophical implications of historical seriality was no more than an exercise in logic. It was, in practice, guided by a philosophical theory about the nature of substitution. My main criticism of Lévi-Strauss's structuralism in its application to our understanding of mythology is not that it is wrong, but that it is deficient. There is nothing wrong in a structuralist interpretation of myth and in some cases it may even have a limited use. My real reservation is due to the fact that the structuralist method is insufficient and tells us considerably less than we can know. Structuralism is aware of and makes great play with the fact that myths come in series, and contends, as the idealistic coherence theory of truth used to do, that the meaning of the series depends on the relationship of the signs to each other rather than on the relationship of each single sign to a fact. But since it neglects the historical nature of this seriality, it sees every member of the series as a mere repetition of a message. If people had sharper ears, the structuralist seems to be saying, they would not have to tell each other the same story quite so often. In other words, each variation of the theme is a mere repetition and can be substituted without loss or gain for every other variation. In this respect, though in this respect only, structuralism does not differ from countless other methods of interpreting myths. Each repetition, whether it is more general or more specific, is treated as a mere substitution the order of which is of no importance. Nothing can be learnt from the order in which a general substitution stands to a less general substitution, or a specific substitution, to a less specific one. Or rather, what can be learnt from a consideration of the order in which the substitutions stand to one another has nothing to do with the growing specification of content apparent in the temporal order of substitutions, but is concerned solely with the formal order in which one substitution stands to another. Structuralism simply discovers in the various substitutions that order which it has imposed upon the substitutions in the process of sorting them into an order. It comes up with the finding that the order is the order that was used in ordering the substitutions.

The observation that myths form historical series leads, however, to a very different theory of the significance of substitution. In this theory every substitution is both necessary and irreversible because it presents the old theme in a more specialised shape. As time passes, substitutions take place. They do not necessarily occur in the same society or in the same place. This much is admitted by structuralism. But the substituted version stands to the version it is substituted for as a symbol, not as a sign. A sign merely duplicates of the thing it signifies and were it not for the fact that the sign is often briefer and more easily communicable than the thing it signifies, one might take it that the substitution of a sign for the thing it signifies is redundant. In any case, it can be dispensed with without loss of meaning and be replaced by the thing it signifies. A symbol is an altogether different kind of substitute. A symbol is more specific and precise in its meaning than the thing it symbolises. Whereas the sign means the thing it signifies and the thing signified is the meaning of the sign, the symbol does not stand in such a simple relationship to the thing it symbolises. Since the symbol has a more specific meaning than the thing it symbolises, the thing symbolised benefits from a feedback and receives a new and more specific meaning from its symbol than it originally possessed. Thing and sign are freely interchangeable. But thing and symbol are not. A thing is the meaning of its *sign*; but a symbol is the meaning of its *thing*. The sign *derives* its meaning from the thing it stands for; the symbol *bestows* meaning on the thing it symbolises. The substitution of the symbol for a thing is therefore irreversible and since the feedback bestows a more specific meaning on the thing symbolised, the substitution is necessary for establishing the more special meaning of the thing symbolised. As a result one cannot say that the thing symbolised is the meaning of the symbol but only that the symbol is the meaning of the thing symbolised. The word 'sheep' is a sign for the animal and means the animal : but the symbol 'spire' is not a sign for a phallus nor is it meant by the phallus. On the contrary : the phallus receives a special meaning when it is symbolised by the spire and the spire is therefore the meaning of the phallus because its meaning is more specific than the meaning of the phallus taken by itself. Since the thing symbolised is not the meaning of the symbol, it is impossible to detect the meaning of the thing symbolised without the symbol. Without the feedback we are in the dark. But this darkness has a chain effect. Since the symbol does not receive its meaning (unlike the sign) from the thing it symbolises, the symbol itself is lacking in meaning unless there is a further symbol for it, i.e. another substitution. Each symbol is part of a series in which the more specific symbol feeds a meaning back to the less specific one and receives a meaning from another still more specific. How then are we to gauge the meaning of a symbol and, for that matter, the meaning of the thing symbolised?

The answer is provided by the phenomenon of historical seriality. Every symbol has a further substitute. That further substitute is more specific than its predecessor, and so forth. One can therefore best gauge the meaning of the symbols in the series by reading the series backwards, that is, by starting with the most specific symbol at the end or top of the series, interpreting the next symbol down as something that is meant by the more specific symbol above it and so forth, until one reaches the bottom or beginning of the series. The symbol at the top will carry its meaning more patently on its face than the symbols at the bottom. The most fruitful method of interpretation, therefore, is neither to seek to replace all substitutions by the thing substituted, as naturalistic methods are wont to do; nor to consider all substitutions as mere repetitions, as structuralism does; but to consider the substitutions as necessary and irreversible and to interpret the meaning of the whole series of substitutions backwards by reading it in the light of the most specified of the series of substitutions. The philosophical consequences of the historical seriality of myths for psychology and ontology are, therefore, worked out consistently in terms of this theory of the special nature of substitution.

Thus we come to another layer. The book owes its existence to the desire to 'defend ancient springs'. Mythology leads us back not only to the most ancient but also to the deepest springs of the human mind. The wish for a correct interpretation of mythology is therefore not just an academic or intellectual exercise. It stems from the concern to keep our lines of communication with the centre clear and untarnished. This concern is shared by Lévi-Strauss, but structuralism's application is not sufficient to keep access to the depths open. Structuralism makes great capital of its implication that the modern mind's logic is identical with the logic of the primitive mind. But the identity is in method and structure of operation and tells nothing of the content, and blithely disregards the mind's urges towards reaching greater precision of self-definition. It overlooks the fact that the phases of the mind's history are not just an accumulation of substitutions. After functionalism, structuralism is today enjoying a great vogue. An examination of its deficiencies and the discovery of an alternative is all the more urgent because the material pressures of modern urban life all conspire to bar that access. The temptation to settle for a logically plausible, if inefficient, method is doubly great because that method, through its very deficiency, is so readily compatible with the barriers created by the materialistic and utilitarian preoccupations which dominate our life and with the cybernetics we have come to use in their pursuit. Inevitably, the book thus becomes also a contribution both to the Philosophy of Religion and to Metaphysics.

The book owes its immediate existence to an invitation by my colleague, Professor J. Pouwer, to communicate my thoughts and doubts on Lévi-Strauss to his Seminar in Anthropology. I also wish to thank Eric Schwimmer for much helpful criticism of the sections on structuralism. I am grateful to the Research Fund and the Publications Fund of the Victoria University of Wellington whose generous support made possible the writing and publication of the book. I also wish to thank Janet Paul for thinking up the title and the University's Reference Librarians, Miss Clark and Mrs Freed, for their patience and ingenuity.

ONE

INTRODUCTION

Almost as far back as one can remember, men have been especially interested in their mythology. It was sensed at first, more than clearly understood, that these mysterious tales, many of which were on the face of it hardly credible, contained either a secret message or enshrined a hidden meaning and that if one could decipher or interpret them, one would reach a truth which was normally beyond one's reach. The study of mythology, it was believed, would reveal a universal truth about man or nature or God, or possibly about all three. The more people learnt of one another, the clearer it became that mythology was a universal phenomenon and that many myths appeared in different cultures at different times either in the same form or with a similar content. Mythology, it gradually emerged, was a body of lore shared by all of mankind and this more than anything else, confirmed the suspicion that it enshrined general truths.

It would be no exaggeration to say that the work of Sir James Frazer was the ultimate and most splendid culmination of this belief. His systematic exploration of the mythology of countless peoples and countless ages was based on the old assumption. Unfortunately it was heavily marred by Frazer's discipleship of Comte, his consequent dislike of metaphysics and religion and his conviction that mankind progressed from magic to religion and from religion to science. Put at a disadvantage by his debt to Comte, Frazer's work and reputation received another, fatal, blow from the growth of functionalism. Under the leadership of Malinowski and Radcliffe-Brown, one student of mythology after another declared that myths, like ritual and economic and social institutions, performed a specific function in the society in which they were being cultivated and that whatever meaning they had could only be grasped by a functional analysis. Such a functional analysis had to relate them to social and economic institutions, to kinship and *mores*. Myths, handled in this manner, could not yield or reveal eternal truths about man and cosmos any more than patrilineal descent can reveal an eternal truth. With this onslaught, which proved in many ways a fruitful approach to the understanding of especially primitive societies, the old tradition of mythological study which had culminated in Frazer received its death-blow. This was all the more regrettable as, ironically, Frazer had been on the point of bringing about a most fruitful and promising *rapprochement* between the study of mythology and traditional theology. Frazer had remarked once that if the story of Christ is so similar to the practices and beliefs of primitive pagan religions, there cannot be much truth in it. Unbeknown to him, this observation can be stood on its head. If the story of Christ, one might rejoin, is so similar to the practices of ancient and primitive religions, it must of necessity enshrine a profound truth. But when functionalism discredited the Frazerian approach, the theologians, who had only just been beginning to join issue with Frazer, withdrew. They heaved a sigh of relief and continued to pursue their own intellectually inbred debates as of old. The greatest innovation in modern theology, the demythologisation proposed by Bultmann, partly as a result of the blow dealt to the Frazerian tradition by functionalism, was not able to draw upon the insights reached by universal comparative mythology but had to confine itself for the deciphering of Christian mythology to the rather narrow and turgidly phrased statements of a German philosopher who, to boot, eventually joined the Nazi movement. How much more fruitful could Bultmann's method have been, had he been able to avail himself with confidence of techniques other than the proclamation that the whole of Christian mythology was an ancient, groping attempt to express the truths put forward by Martin Heidegger. By contrast, it is equally regrettable that the great interest in mythology generated by C. G. Jung and so vigorously followed up by his many followers in the *Eranos* Year Books has remained so innocent of systematic techniques of interpretation. Jung spotted very perceptively that there is a parallelism between dream images and mythology. He formed the theory that dreams reflect developments or blockages of physical energy, and since he thought he knew how psychic energy behaves throughout the life-span of every individual, he was able to interpret dreams as symptoms of blocked aspirations or impending developments, as the case may be. And then he simply ransacked the whole of mythology and concluded that any mythical image has the same meaning as the dream image it is similar to. Conversely, he believed that any dreamer may avail himself of any mythical image according to the needs of his psychic energy by drawing up mythical images from the 'collective unconscious'. Whatever the therapeutic efficiency of such an approach, this catholicism cannot recommend itself to the serious student of mythology. There is much wisdom and beauty in the contributions to the *Eranos* Year Books; but they are singularly lacking in consistent theory.

Perhaps for the sake of Jung's and Bultmann's own fruitful ideas, if for nothing else, it is therefore necessary to welcome the new lease of life which the universal science of mythology, as distinct from the functional interpretation of myth, has received from the work of Lévi-Strauss. Lévi-Strauss is a man of such wide erudition and practical experience in the study of primitive people, as well as a man formidable in argument, that his revival of the universal science of mythology has commanded attention. A quarter of a century ago any approach which treated mythology as a universal language was laughed out of court by the functionalists. Today, with Lévi-Strauss's backing, such attempts are listened to with serious interest. For this reason it is doubly important to subject Lévi-Strauss's own methods and practices in the interpretation of mythology to close scrutiny lest the revival of interest be once again discredited by exhibiting too close and dogmatic a reliance on certain accidental presuppositions, just as Frazer suffered through his dependence on Comte.

One is forced to concede, at the outset, that the functionalists have one great advantage over all other interpreters of mythology. In a functionalist approach, the question of the independent meaning of myth does not arise. A myth or a whole system of mythology *means* the function it has in the social system as a whole, nothing more and nothing less. The functionalist does therefore not have to worry about a method of interpretation to bring out the meaning of mythology other than looking at it in its social setting. But if one is willing to consider myths as a product of the universal human mind one has to offer both a theory of the meaning of these tales and

3

a theory of interpreting them. By the nature of the case, the two can never really be distinct. To Frazer and Freud, to Jung and the older cosmological school, the meaning of the myth was – to paraphrase an old positivistic adage – the method of its interpretation. That is to say, they all postulated what myths meant and then fashioned a way of interpreting them to show that they meant indeed precisely what they were postulated to mean. The functionalist does not have to decode; and he is therefore innocent of this circularity. But the interpreter of myth as a universal phenomenon is bound to decode and the first difficulty he faces is that his method of decoding is governed by his theory of the meaning of mythology. Frazer believed that myths were a primitive form of thinking about the control of nature, now superseded by science. When he decoded his myths, he found that the message they conveyed was indeed a very primitive one. Jung believed that myths are like dreams and convey messages and warnings about conflicts in the psyche; and when he decoded them, he found that they conveyed such warnings and messages. There is no obvious way of proving this circularity wrong. But the fact that the argument is usually circular must make it suspect and it would therefore be a great advantage if one could devise a way of interpreting myth non-functionally and avoid such circularity. The only way of achieving this seems to be to probe whether the structure of a mythological system (i.e. a collection of tales which hang together in form or content or both) itself does perhaps embody a method of interpretation. If one could discover a method of interpretation which is inherent in the mythology itself, one could at least claim that mythology reveals or exhibits its own meaning and obviate the need for decoding.

TWO

A CRITIQUE
OF STRUCTURALISM

Let us first of all take a critical look at the principles of Lévi-Strauss, the great restorer of the non-functional approach. The basic principle of his approach is that 'myths think themselves in men'. By this he means that myths are not stories which are made up voluntarily and arbitrarily but that they have a compulsive hold on the human mind and manifest themselves in the mind. They are some of the fundamental forms in which the human mind thinks. The second principle is that myths must be interpreted serially and that they cannot reveal their meaning when considered as single stories. It is important to be clear as to the implication of serial interpretation. Lévi-Strauss thinks that each myth must be broken up into its constituent phases and that these phases or episodes must be considered as a series. Furthermore, he postulates that these episodes exhibit a similarity in structure and that the episodes must be taken to be a series of messages with the same meaning – the sum total of episodes being a series of repetitive signals which hammer in the same message, in case people do not get the message the first time. The third principle is that when these episodes are considered serially, one will find that they can be arranged in two columns. The first column will contain episodes which overstress or overrate something; and the second column will contain episodes which underrate or de-value the same thing. In this sense he believes that myths are collections of episodes in which the opposites of institutions or phenomena or judgements are alternately overvalued and undervalued. The fourth and last general principle is the contention that by such alternate undervaluation and overvaluation, the conflict or tension or incompatibility between the two institutions or phenomena is 'resolved'. If, for example, incest and exogamy, autochthony and bisexual procreation, life and death, nature and culture are persistently undervalued and overvalued, people will eventually resign themselves to the fact that their own customs and conventions are half way between the two extremes or are a compromise between the two extremes.

It seems impossible to accept all these four principles uncritically. But at the same time, the criticism of each of the principles is different so that one cannot accept or reject the system of principles as a whole.

The first principle seems acceptable *in toto* and is, in fact, no more or less than a statement of the non-functional interpretation of mythology. It invites us to consider mythology as a form of human thought and by implication it explains the stubborn hold of mythology on the human mind. The second principle of serial interpretation is also basically sound. It is not as original as Lévi-Strauss or his followers think. Indeed, it has a very honourable and distinguished ancestry. When the Fathers of the Church had to reconcile the Old Testament with the New, it struck them that the stories of the Old and the stories of the New come in series and that one should consider the earlier stories to have 'pre-figured' the later ones. There is no need to discuss the theological premises of this view; but it is important to note that they took it that myths and their meanings are not particular phenomena. The arrangement of these series depends of course on the discovery of structure. One can arrange myths in series only when they have the same structure. Eventually the same approach was used in order to reconcile Homeric myths with Neo-Platonism and the historical events of the Old Testament (literal interpretation) with the ethical commands (moral interpretation) of the Christian religion, and with its theology (allegorical interpretation) and its mysticism (anagogical interpretation). For that matter, artists have frequently exploited the phenomenon of structure by providing series of new images. Manet, for instance, took a sixteenth-century engraving by Marcantonio Raimondi of the Judgement of Paris – or more exactly one part of it – as a model for his notorious *Le Déjeuner sur l'herbe*[1] and eventually Picasso painted a whole collection of canvasses with the same structure. The literary exploitation of mythical themes is well known and depends on the same insight; the recurrence in literature of the Tristan and Iseult theme, the Faustus theme or the Don Giovanni theme need only be alluded to. Freud insisted that dreams have to be interpreted as a series and cannot reveal their meaning when considered in isolation from one another. The whole exploration of the unconscious depends on the realisation that there are phenomena which are quite dissimilar but which exhibit the same structure. How else could one demonstrate that a tree can be a phallic symbol and that often, when people talk of trees they mean, though they are not aware of it, phalluses? One could even go so far as to argue that the only evidence we have for the presence of the unconscious mind is our awareness of similarities in structure. For since we cannot, by definition, be aware of the *unconscious* desire to think of the phallus, we can only conclude that when a tree is mentioned it means a phallus, because we are aware of the structural affinity between a tree and phallus.

Perhaps one has to grant that if this line of thought is pursued too tenaciously, we are in danger of doing injustice to the novelty of Lévi-Strauss's structuralism, for as Piaget has sensibly insisted[2] 'structure' must be defined more narrowly than 'form'.

Nevertheless, there is no denying that Lévi-Strauss puts the importance of the series to a novel use.[3] To begin with, his insistence on the importance of the series stresses that there is a great difference between mere form and structure – a fact of which many earlier writers had only been dimly aware. Form is the opposite of content and it is possible to define the form of a story without looking at other stories of the same structure. But when one insists that structure can only be understood by considering a whole series of structurally identical stories, one provides a definition of structure. The definition is that the structure is an essential part of the content. One can say that a story in which a man kills a chthonic being and a story in which a man kills a celestial being have the same form. But one cannot say that they have the same structure. For the structure of the first story is much more like the structure of the story in which a snake eats a root than like the structure of the second story. If one confines one's attention to one story only, it is usually impossible to point at the difference between its form and its structure. It is possible to isolate its form from its content; but it is not possible to identify its structure. Furthermore, there is something relatively novel in Lévi-Strauss's method of breaking up myths into single small episodes and in his discovery that these single episodes can be arranged in two structurally opposite columns. And finally, there is something new in Lévi-Strauss's contention that the episodes repeat one and the same message and hammer it in by such repetition. There remains, however, the question as to who is sending the messages and to whom they are being sent. If one answers that they are being sent by the older generation to the younger generation, one must ask why it is considered necessary to send such messages. The answer must contain a reference to a purpose, to a function. But if this is the only answer, Lévi-Strauss is in great danger of putting himself squarely back into functionalism. One must therefore consider the possibility that the message is being sent by the unconscious mind, possibly by the collective unconscious mind, to the conscious mind. But if this is the answer to the question as to who is sending the message to whom, there arises a further problem. Why must we think, in this case, of messages at all? Does Lévi-Strauss mean that the unconscious provides us with information about itself? If so, why the roundabout manner? Why does the unconscious not simply make itself known as it is?

In order to understand this correctly it is necessary to look at Lévi-Strauss's principles of interpretation in their general philosophical framework. Many philosophers have stressed that the whole of the world is a seamless web in constant flux and that any sub-division of segments we single out for observation, as objects or as distinct entities to which we can give a name, are artificially analysed. Philosophers vary in their reaction to this insight. Bergson reacted violently against it and denounced the human intellect which is the author of these artificially analysed segments. He insisted that we ought to try to intuit the seamless web as it flows or endures, and refrain from segmenting it. Kant, on the other hand, although he did not deny the existence of the *noumenal* world, thought it perfectly proper that the human mind should use categories to analyse and sub-divide it. He explained that such analytical sub-divisions would never falsify or distort our experience, for our experience itself is filtered through the same categories and therefore will always correspond to the sub-divisions and segments our mind has introduced. In this approach, it is, however, important to be aware of the categories and forms our understanding uses in order to sort experience into separate fragments and segments. As is well known, Hegel attempted to improve on Kant's theory by devising a special logic which would do greater justice to the fluid web of the *noumenal* world by being itself rather fluid and seamless: he invented dialectical logic, according to which the denial of A eventually transformed itself into the assertion of A. He thought that in this way logical reasoning would eventually present the world as it really was and not make it appear in the static shape of Kantian categories and Kantian forms of understanding.

Lévi-Strauss's basic position in regard to this matter is thoroughly Kantian. He is aware of the seamless web but believes that our understanding analytically and artificially segments it and sub-divides it. He is, however, non-Kantian in his non-psychological approach to the manner in which the segmentation is performed. Instead of sharing Kant's belief that time and space are the filters of human experience, that is, neuro-psychological processes, and that experiences are further categorised in the brain, he argues that the human mind is dominated by a fundamental and very simple logic of segmentation. It works as follows. We perceive, for instance, a melody played by an orchestra as a seamless web of sound. But it can be broken up both vertically and horizontally. If one looks at an orchestra score, one can read it vertically as a set of harmonies; and horizontally, as a melody. Now Lévi-Strauss observes that one can look upon almost anything in the same manner. The way in which we construct our houses can be analysed similarly. We can arrange in a vertical column all the separate elements such as iron-roofs, tile-roofs, slats, straw-webbing, fibre-glass sheets. In the next column we have stairs, lifts, ladders, that is all devices which connect a lower floor to a higher floor. And so on. In the horizontal columns we have the series which contain the actual way in which each house is put together: a fibre-glass roof, a lift, etc. The same can be done for clothing. The vertical columns will contain first, hats, berets, hoods, caps; next, vests, jackets, pullovers, cardigans, jerseys; and so forth. The horizontal column will contain the way in which any one person is actually dressed: hat, jersey, shirt, trousers, etc. This is all almost common-sense and anybody who has ever been to a restaurant will have noticed that most menus are written in precisely this style. The vertical column lists first the entrées, then the main courses, then the sweets. And horizontal columns will present any actual menu chosen: fish, roast-pork, apple-pie.

At the beginning of this century it was discovered by students of language that one can analyse the seamless web of speech in the same way. Instead of absorbing speech as a seamless succession of sounds, it is possible to break it up into parts and order the parts in vertical and horizontal columns. The vertical columns will contain, in separate columns, the separate words which are available. And the horizontal columns will contain the sentences which are actually spoken in any one particular language. So that we get, vertically, lists of words belonging to the same category; and, horizontally, chains of words which we call meaningful sentences.

Lévi-Strauss's originality lies in bringing all these observations together. He observes that the activity of the human mind is basically to be compared with that of a *bricoleur,* a man who collects odd items and assembles them into a more or less useful object. The human mind looks at the several vertical columns, chooses one piece from each column and then makes a chain out of the several pieces. Here, then, we have a general account, non-Kantian, of the manner in which the seamless web of the *noumenal* world is analysed and in which the segments are assembled into the flow of speech, melodies, houses, menus, etc. Furthermore, Lévi-Strauss has drawn our attention to the fact that the phenomenon of language is simply one more part of the *noumenal* world which can be analysed according to the same principle. The final and general conclusion is that, although the seamless web of reality cannot be grasped as such, the world we live in and understand and talk about, as well as the manner in which we talk about it, all exhibit the same structure. In Lévi-Strauss's thinking, therefore, structure tends to occupy the place occupied in Kant by the categories and the forms of understanding. It would take us too far to attempt to assess the relative merits of the competing accounts of how we break up the totality of experience and reassemble it into intelligible wholes, but there is no denying that we have here a *prima facie* viable alternative to the Kantian account. Lévi-Strauss tries to do the same sort of thing which Kant tried to do. In that sense, he is Kantian and opposed both to Hegel and Bergson.

When we now turn to the application of this theory to mythology, we can discern, however, a grave flaw. Myths, Lévi-Strauss plausibly argues, are part of the universe we live in. They can be expected to exhibit the same structure as houses and menus, as language and clothing. Hence his method of breaking them up into episodes and of arranging them in vertical and horizontal columns. The vertical columns will each contain the episodes which tell the same tale (Oedipus killing his father, Eteokles killing his brother); and the horizontal columns will contain the whole story of the myth, assembled by choosing one episode from each column. Given the general system of thought, this method of explaining the composition of myth, or, for that matter, of analysing the myth into its constituent parts, is perfectly acceptable. Myths, in this sense have the same structure as houses, as clothing, as menus, and as language. So far, so good.

It so happened, however, that the analysis of language was chronologically the first discovery of structure. And we have Lévi-Strauss's own word that his general account of structure was derived from the particular account of structure in language. It seems – and this is unfortunate – that Lévi-Strauss has allowed this chronology to run away with his arguments. Theoretically speaking, he ought to have argued that myths and houses, menus and clothing exhibit the same structure as language and that we make the one intelligible by the same methods by which we make all the others intelligible. But in fact he argued that the phenomenon of language was paradigmatic and that all other systems of structure (houses, menus, clothing, myths) are therefore 'languages'. One might even have accepted this as a form of speech, as a metaphor, were it not for the fact that Lévi-Strauss goes further. Strictly speaking, the metaphor can be turned round. If language has the same structure as clothing and houses, then we ought to be able to say that language is houses as well as that houses are a language. But Lévi-Strauss insists that language is the model and that myths and menus, clothing and houses are structured as languages and *are* 'languages'. And at this point, the argument becomes false. With this argument one is committed to the view that myths and houses *convey* a meaning or message or communication even as language does. On Lévi-Strauss's own theory, a language has the same structure as houses and clothing and myths; but there is nothing to prove that language is paradigmatic and that we are therefore justified in seeing myths and houses and clothing as 'languages'. The programme of decoding mythology is therefore not only questionable, but seems to be based on the erroneous assumption that for some reason or other, if all structured systems, the system of language is paradigmatic. It is one thing to understand the phenomenon of structure as a replica or analogy of the structure of language; but quite another thing to argue that, because one's understanding of language first suggested the idea, language occupies a basic position in the whole system of structures.

When we look at the third principle of binary opposition, one must have grave doubts. There is no question (and Lévi-Strauss has taken care to make this explicit) that Lévi-Strauss is reacting strongly against Lévy-Bruhl's view that primitive man has pre-logical thoughts. Lévi-Strauss believes that the notion of pre-logical thinking is part of the doctrine of gradual evolution of man from the animal kingdom. Lévi-Strauss believes that, against the doctrine of evolution, there is an absolute break between nature and culture, between the animal realm and the realm of man. He is therefore eager to demonstrate that primitive man, no matter *how* primitive and *how* early, was capable of the same kind of logical thinking as we are and that that logical thinking was not really primitive and pre-logical. The simplest way of demonstrating the all-pervasiveness of logical thinking is to show that our form of reasoning that something is either A or non-A is the absolute paradigm of all thinking. Hence Lévi-Strauss's predilection for binary oppositions and his famous theory of Totemism.

By the nature of the case it is impossible to falsify the theory that all thinking, sophisticated advanced thinking as well as primitive thinking, is of this logical type. It is impossible to conceive of any phenomenon which, if one could point at it, would prove Lévi-Strauss's contention wrong. But it does not therefore necessarily follow that he is right. On the contrary. The mere fact that we know from his own words that he is reacting strongly to Lévy-Bruhl makes us wary; for we know on his own testimony that he is partisan and therefore predisposed towards the discovery that primitive thought is as logical as our own thought. Furthermore, Lévi-Strauss is here caught in the old dilemma of all non-functional mytho-logical interpretation: his method is the meaning. When he therefore proposes to arrange episodes in two binarily opposite columns he is not demonstrating that all myths must be thus arranged. He is merely proving that it can be done. When he comes up with the argument that myths *mean* to exhibit such binary oppositions, he is arguing in a circle.

The fourth principle, which maintains that myths serve the purpose of resolving the conflict between nature and culture, incest and exogamy, and so forth, presents even greater problems. For if this principle is accepted, one is forced to the conclusion that Lévi-Strauss is not nearly so far removed from functionalism as he thinks. If we accept the notion of resolution, we must immediately ask for whom the conflict exists and for whom it is reconciled.

In the case of the conflict between life and death, one could well believe that the conflict is universal and that it exists for all men in so far as they are conscious of the fact that all life ends in death. But when we come to the conflict between nature and culture, we cannot easily conclude that this conflict is equally universal. For there are societies in which the distinction between nature and culture is not an absolute one. On Lévi-Strauss's own theory, in such societies there ought to be an absence of myths which alternately overvalue and undervalue nature and culture. If this is so – and it might be difficult to prove this not only as a matter of statistics but also as a matter of interpretation (what do some people mean by 'nature' and by 'culture'?) – it follows that the myths about the conflict between nature and culture pertain to certain societies and not to others and have a distinct *function* in those to which they pertain. And if this is not a functional interpretation of myth one would like to know what is. And the same argument must apply, with even greater force, to the opposition between incest and exogamy. On a more general level, one must have serious doubts in regard to the very notion of 'resolution'. Is it really credible that the conflict between nature and culture, and for that matter any conflict, is 'resolved' if one is subjected from early childhood onwards to repetitions of stories in which culture is either overvalued or undervalued? Is it not more likely that one's awareness of conflict is increased by such exaggerations? By overstressing and understressing culture and nature alternately, one is made more aware of the conflict, not less aware. It is difficult to see therefore how mythology resolves contradictories. But here again, the circularity problem appears. If the method of interpretation is based upon distinguishing episodes which understress from episodes which overstress, one cannot really argue convincingly that the meaning of myths is to make people aware of the contradictoriness of the phenomena overstressed and the phenomena understressed; for that would be to say that the method *is* the meaning, and the medium, the message. It is true that in a different context MacLuhan *has* argued that the medium is the message. But there are good reasons for thinking that MacLuhan is wrong. Nobody can deny that the medium *does*, among other things, 'message'. But there are other messages contained in the medium. And when Lévi-Strauss comes up with the finding that the meaning of myth is the resolution of the binary contradiction which is inherent in its structure, this conclusion must be very suspect, for it does reduce the meaning to the method of interpretation. It is true that there is a difference between being suspect and being wrong; and that it is possible that the method is *indeed* the meaning. But the argument employed by Lévi-Strauss strongly reminds one of other such homologous forms of discovery. An example of this is Freud's desire to solve the riddle of the sphinx. He made the discovery that the sphinx was a mother-figure and produced the answer that the solution to the riddle is that we want to solve the riddle, i.e. that we want to unveil our mother. He may be right. But one's doubts are not allayed by the realisation that his theory is homologous, that is, that the answer *is* the theory.

If one has varying degrees of reservation about the different principles of Lévi-Strauss's interpretation of mythology, these reservations all seem to lead to one ultimate consideration. Lévi-Strauss aims to decode myths. He proceeds on the assumption that mythology is a language which is not understood and that it ought to be translated into a language which can be understood. It is as if he were arguing that mythology is like the original Greek text of Homer, which most people today cannot understand, and that it ought therefore to be translated into modern English. The real crux of the matter is whether he is justified in this assumption.

It is doubtful whether it can be possible to reach any agreement on this question. For this question not only concerns the nature of mythology but also the nature of language. It is well known that Lévi-Strauss believes that language is a method of exchanging information and one of his most ingenious contributions to the study of man is his generalisation from this belief. He generalises and argues that, since all social and cultural relations are forms of exchange, they are forms of language. It would take too long to go into the justification of this generalisation. But for our present purposes it is important to point out that in many important senses a language is not just a method of exchanging information. In fact, one could go so far as to maintain that any human language is considerably impoverished if it is solely used for the exchange of information or the communication of messages; and I am often highly suspicious of all linguistic exchanges because I know that it is possible thus to impoverish them and to use language, among other things, also for purposes of communication. Words, after all, are things. They are objects like trees and houses, like people and furniture. They can be used as codes which convey messages. But it does not follow that any of these objects are *nothing but* codes. Every child which learns to speak uses its first words not for communication but as ends in themselves. The child will point to a car and repeat 'car' a thousand times even when it must be fully aware that the adult watching has got the message. The explanation is that the child is not concerned with conveying a message to the adult but takes pleasure from enunciating the word. The word is an end in itself. It does not signify the car but is one more object over and above the car. The child, by pronouncing the word 'car', is beginning to lose interest in the car and taking pride and interest in the new object, the word 'car'. There is no strength in the objection that children are stupid and are misusing language. For the whole phenomenon of poetry, the fact that there is poetry as well as prose, is based on the same principle. A poem is a structure of words; not a means of communicating something which could, in fact, be communicated more clearly and directly and unequivocally in prose. W. H. Auden once pointed out that the acid test of poetic sensibility is whether one can derive joy from a recital of the names of Paris underground railway stations.[4] For that matter, it has been found that a mathematical calculus or the calculus of propositions as developed in Russell's *Principia Mathematica* is a more precise and unambiguous vehicle for communicating messages and information than the richly nuanced speech of Shakespeare or Rilke. And it has even been argued plausibly that in so far as language conveys nothing but information, our daily usage of English is superfluously rich and that it can be reduced to 'basic English' and that 'basic' is fully adequate for carrying out the function of conveying information. If language is a code for conveying information rather than an object in its own right why do we so stubbornly adhere to the complex usage of our languages and why do we not reduce them to the calculus of propositions or to basic English? Poetry, Wallace Stevens said, 'is part of the *res* itself and not about it'.[5]

The answer must be fairly clear. Language is much more than a code. And, by the same token, myths are much more than a code. Myths, like words and sentences, exist as ends in themselves, and it makes no more sense to ask for the purpose of a language and mythology than it makes to ask for the purpose of trees. This does not mean that language and myth cannot be used for certain purposes even as trees can be used for shelter or firewood. But such purposes are not primary purposes.

There is one further argument against treating myths as a language and this argument, if anything, is more final than the previous one. It is well known that one of the remarkable things about language is the fact that one can produce an unlimited number of different sentences with an extremely limited number of words and rules. In mythology the reverse is true. The sum total of all myths can be reduced to a very finite number of motifs. In fact it is one of the commonplaces of the study of mythology to remark on the comparative poverty of the mythological imagination. But the materials used for mythology are well-nigh infinite. One could therefore argue that, whatever operation is at work in the use of language, the opposite operation seems to be at work in creation of myth.

If we then take the reservation in regard to the circularity of Lévi-Strauss's interpretation (i.e. the method equals the meaning) together with our general reservation in regard to the purpose of language and myth, we come to the conclusion that it is wrong to look upon myth as a language which has to be decoded; that is to say, as a system of communication which can be translated without loss into another system. The circularity could, of course, be taken care of by a return to functionalism. But this remedy is not available to Lévi-Strauss. When, on the contrary, he speaks of 'decoding', he merely reinforces the circularity, because even if one granted that there is good sense in decoding, one must come to the conclusion that decoding means translation. And if one translates a myth into another 'language' one does not get at its meaning but simply translates it. If one translates a French text into English, one does not uncover its meaning; for one could not argue that the French text *meant* the English text and that it was originally written in French by mistake or some form of perversity and that it was all along destined to be revealed in its English meaning. If one believes in decoding, one is destined to endless efforts at decoding, for any language can be translated into another language and so forth *ad infinitum*. There is no *absolute* language into which it can be translated and which would be the ultimate meaning of the original.

THREE

THE AMBIVALENCE
OF THE DISTINCTION BETWEEN
STRUCTURALISM AND
FUNCTIONALISM

The close examination of the reservations which one must have in regard to Lévi-Strauss's programme has been fruitful in that it has drawn attention to the difficulties encountered when one wishes to avoid a functional interpretation by likening myths to other systems such as clothing and houses and menus and language. Each particular type of clothing or housing or myth or language can be interpreted functionally as part of a total culture. But Lévi-Strauss attempts to look upon these systems as languages.

One could almost try to analyse the problem in his own terms. If one arranges the various phenomena in vertical columns, one will find that these columns list houses, myths, language, political institutions, kinship systems, etc. And if one reads horizontally, one will come up with a chain of functionally interrelated phenomena in any one particular culture: a certain type of house, a certain type of clothes, a certain system of myth and a certain system of kinship. The grand debate whether we should look at societies functionally or whether we should rather look upon the separate elements and link them with comparable elements from other cultures is, therefore, essentially a non-debate. A structural analysis of the materials shows that one can read them vertically as well as horizontally, whichever way one wishes or considers useful. For that matter, one can look at the whole question functionally and come up with the view that our method – which leads to the view that functional and non-functional interpretation are equally viable – is functionally related to our modern cosmopolitan theory-oriented culture. The pursuit of structural interpretations is functionally explicable in societies which have a high degree of mobility, offer a high level of freedom of choice, and possess both museums and libraries of ethnography. It is therefore not possible to maintain that structuralism is more fundamental than functionalism

because structuralism shows that we may choose between structuralism and functionalism: if we turn the whole argument round, we see
that we get a functional appreciation of the structural method which
teaches us that we may choose as we wish; either a functional or a
structural approach. It seems therefore that structuralism can justify
functionalism; and functionalism, structuralism – always assuming, of
course, that we are speaking from the vantage point of our particular,
modern, theory-minded, cosmopolitan society; which is the vantage
point from which we are, in fact, speaking.

One can also put this in a different way. We always have a
problem when we want to state what precisely it is that we wish to
understand and explain. When we apply functionalism from the
vantage point of our own society, which we know to be very un-
integrated and non-functional, we are really saying that we wish to
understand primitive societies as essentially different from our own
society. There is, therefore, a certain condescension in the use of
functionalism. We know that our modern, western, urban, mass
societies operate, on the whole, in a very non-functional manner. We
have religious beliefs that are not closely related in a functional
manner with our steel-industry; and we have a wide variety of sexual
customs which are not strictly functionally related to our methods of
rearing children; and so forth. Nor is our democratic political system a
function of our literary tastes. When we seek to understand primitive
societies in which customs and beliefs, economics and politics are
functionally related, we are understanding them as societies that are
profoundly different from our own. Our understanding, therefore, consists in pointing at the differences. The application of functionalism is
not likely to build a bridge between our own social orders and those of
primitive peoples but must result in making us constantly aware of
basic differences between us and them. Now take structuralism.
Structuralism is, on the contrary, concerned to show that primitive
societies operate basically on the same system on which our own
societies operate. We order our social relations and customs, our
economics and beliefs, by distinguishing A from non-A. So do they.
Hence structuralism seeks to understand by building a bridge. Far
from being condescending, it falls over backwards to stress that the
differences between the Amazon Indians and modern New Yorkers
are minimal.

We conclude then that the understanding provided by functionalism is due to the way in which it brings out the differences between us and them. The understanding provided by structuralism consists in the fact that the similarities between us and them are stressed. Now it so happens that in so far as we can see our modern mass societies in functional terms, we can see that the structural method is functionally related to our technological culture, the primacy of logical reasoning and cybernetics, to computing and democracy and empirical science. Its application not only builds a bridge between our societies and those of more primitive people but can also be said to be functionally related to the institutions of our own societies. If we look at our own societies from the point of functionalism, we see that the appropriate scientific method for the understanding of our own societies as well as of more primitive societies is structuralism. Functionalism therefore, in our modern society, justifies or gives primacy to structuralism. But here we have a seeming paradox. If the recommendation that we employ structuralism depends on a functional view of our own modern society, then the primacy of structuralism is due to an even greater primacy of functionalism, for it is only functionalism which commends, in our special circumstances, the employment of structuralism.

The paradox becomes even more complex when we consider that one can also turn the matter upside down. We have said that one can establish the primacy of structuralism as a valid method for understanding societies on the basis of functionalism, for structural understanding is functionally integrated with all our other institutions. But we have also argued that functionalism explains by stressing the differences between our own societies and primitive societies. Hence functionalism and structuralism are related to one another as A to non-A. It follows, therefore, that the employment of functionalism for the understanding of primitive societies is structurally intelligible from the point of view of our own modern, non-primitive societies. Here, then, we find that functionalism is recommended by structuralism. Whereas before we reached the conclusion that functionalism commends or justifies structuralism, we now come to the conclusion that structuralism commends and justifies functionalism.

In view of these different conclusions, we must content ourselves with the insight that neither method constitutes a royal way, let alone an absolute. On the contrary, the one justifies the other; and the other the one.

Be this as it may. The examination of the difficulties encountered by structuralism will lead to the conclusion that it is not really acceptable to interpret mythology non-functionally by comparing it to other 'languages'. If we wish to persist with an alternative to functionalism, and there is no reason why we should not persist, we must therefore be more circumspect and probe whether mythology is not a system of stories which will yield up a meaning internally. By this is meant that we should inquire whether myths can be made to exhibit their meanings autonomously. If they do, if they carry their own meaning more or less clearly within them, there is no need to wrest a meaning from them by comparing them with other 'languages'.

FOUR

THE PHENOMENON OF TYPOLOGY

The best start for our inquiry is a criticism of Lévi-Strauss's *approach* to myth. Lévi-Strauss has a peculiarly unhistorical approach. He takes a myth as a myth and never asks about its origins, and if not about its origins, about its ancestors. Functionalism, too, is notoriously uninterested in the historical origins of myths. But even the functionalist has to admit that as a matter of historical fact, every myth or every part of every myth or every piece of lore that has gone into a myth, must have had its actual origin in a particular socio-economic setting of a particular culture. The functionalist is at pains to insist that such origin sheds no light on the meaning of myth and that that meaning depends on the manner in which the myth functions in a particular society and on the way in which it is functionally interrelated with ways of ritual and of earning a living and of settling political disputes and with kinship structure. The meaning, the functionalist argues, depends on its relation to non-mythical activities. Even so, the functionalist does not deny that myths or several parts of myth, have certain specific historical origins. All he denies is that these origins are relevant to their meanings.

Now Lévi-Strauss, in order to steer clear of functionalism and to avoid its least vestiges, falls over backwards. He not only refuses to look at the way in which a myth functions in any particular socio-economic setting, but also lacks all interest in the historical genesis of myth. In opposition to Lévi-Strauss I am suggesting that we ought to consider first and foremost a myth as a historical phenomenon. By this I do not mean that we ought to investigate the socio-economic genesis of every myth and trace every myth back to its cultural setting. I am arguing that every myth as it is known to us has a history. We know it in some historical form or other. Some myths are known to us as told by very primitive people and other myths are known to us as told by writers who, though highly literary, had access to oral tradition. Other myths are obviously complicated digests of several mythical traditions which were joined and assimilated in the mind of a writer; and other myths, again, are completely divorced from any tradition, oral or written, and are no more than literarily moulded material – moulded for purposes of modern literature or psychology, politics or morals. Lévi-Strauss is strangely neglectful of this aspect of myth and chooses any myth at any one of these stages of treatment, and attributes no importance at all to the fact that these myths are known to us at very different levels of literary treatment. At this point, however, it is important to avoid misunderstanding. Lévi-Strauss is aware that myths have a historical dimension and he always insists that every myth is the sum total of *all* its versions throughout history, and that every myth consists of transmutations and transformations, and that all of these, throughout history, are part of the myth. In this sense, then, he takes history into account. But history here plays a very subordinate and accidental role. It simply so happens that the same myth occurs in many forms. Once it is broken up into its constituent phases, there is no difference between the historical position of one phase and that of another. He agrees that the version of the Oedipus myth as told by Freud is part of the material to be considered. But he does not attribute any importance to the fact that Freud's version is later than Sophocles's and that this time relationship between Sophocles and Freud should make some difference. On the contrary, taken to its logical conclusion, the analysis of myth reaches a point where history annuls itself. This means that although Lévi-Strauss is aware that there is no absolute *authentic* version of any myth from which other versions are so many deviations or by comparison with which other versions are garbled accounts, he does not see this absence of authenticity as a historical phenomenon.

Strictly speaking there is no such thing as the myth of Oedipus or the myth of the dying God. There is Sophocles's story of Oedipus; but there are also a great many, earlier, folk-tales concerned with Oedipus and possibly a myth about a god Oedipus. Alternately, what is the myth of Ulysses? Is it the collection of stories in the *Odyssey* or is it Dante's Ulysses or is it the Ulysses who is conjured up by James Joyce? And what is the myth of the dying God? Are we to take it in some ancient Ugaritic form; or in the stories of Tammuz; or as the

Gospels present it? If the last, then which Gospel? Or are we perhaps to consider it in its medieval shape as we meet it in Abelard's sonnet: 'Solus ad victimam procedis, Domine...' ('Alone to sacrifice Thou goest, Lord...'); or in an earlier medieval version in which it was a ransom sacrifice?

It is true that Lévi-Strauss pays a passing compliment to the historical dimensions of myths when he says that a structural analysis must take into account all versions of any myth and that an analysis of the Oedipus myth, for example, must take into account not only Sophocles but also Freud's version. Unfortunately Lévi-Strauss does not take this insistence very seriously and is high-handed in dismissing its implications, for he goes on to argue that all versions are simply so many variations on one theme. Thus he admits that Freud's version of the Oedipus myth has ceased to be a variation on the theme autochthony *versus* bisexual reproduction, but says that it ought to be understood as a variation on the original theme by reformulating it as a story of how one can be born from two[1]. By this rewriting of Freud, he reduces the Freudian version to a platitude and deprives it of its specific meaning. He also demonstrates that when he says that Freud's version ought to be considered alongside the Sophoclean version and all the other versions that preceded it, he does not really mean what he says. He is willing to consider it alongside the other versions only once he has re-written it.[2] At any rate, this example shows that the only thing that matters to Lévi-Strauss is the theme and that its variations are nothing more than historical accidents and that the location in time of the several versions is irrelevant since they are mere variations on the theme and that, if necessary, they have to be re-written to conform to the theme. Once it is admitted that historical extensions of the theme or of any theme are no more than accidental variations and particular instances of the theme, the whole notion of 'other versions' or of 'variations' becomes really superfluous. Ultimately, therefore, Lévi-Strauss does believe that any myth can be considered as a phenomenon isolated from the versions which precede and succeed it.

The nearest he comes, then, to taking into account that all myths have histories, and that no myth is known to us in an absolute version of which earlier and later versions are so many deviations, is when he repeatedly insists that all known versions of any myth must (or may?) be taken into consideration when one starts decoding it into its constituent sub-themes. But with this postulate, Lévi-Strauss really comes close to abandoning the realm of the empirical study of mythology. For if one indiscriminately may assemble into alternating columns of respective overvaluation and undervaluation any sub-theme culled from any version, there is no reason whatever why one should confine oneself in one's assembly of sub-themes to sub-themes culled from all versions of any one particular myth. If we take Lévi-Strauss's postulate seriously, we can insert sub-themes overstressing incest from the Oedipus myth into the column containing sub-themes overstressing incest taken from the tale of Job or the Buddha myth. In such a case, all we get is collections of sub-themes overstressing incest in one column; and collections of sub-themes underrating incest, in contrasting columns. And since it is possible to overvalue and under-value alternately anything whatever, we will never be at a loss as to what to put into our columns. But, one must conclude, what would such a lack of being at a loss prove? Nothing at all beyond the fact that everything can be either overrated or underrated. But that much we know without recourse to the massive study of myth.

It is strange that G. S. Kirk,[3] one of Lévi-Strauss's most elaborate if sympathetic critics, should go even beyond Lévi-Strauss in his rejec-tion of the historical life of every myth. Kirk seems to believe that myth can best be studied and interpreted in its 'original' form. As an authority on the literature of non-literate peoples, he is very con-scious of the fact that the transmission of stories is subject to vagaries and that changes are being made all the time. But he is of the opinion that, as a result of these changes, the myths are 'heavily polluted' because they show 'marks of progressive remodelling'. I would argue, on the contrary, that such progressive remodelling is neither an anomaly nor a cause for regret. Kirk seems to be unaware that, as a rule, there is method in the changes and that the dis-placement of motifs and accents, the shifts in emphasis and detail, are not due to carelessness, but to design.

Let us therefore do the exact reverse. Let us proceed on the assumption that myths have histories – not in the sense that each myth is linked to a society and culture which has its place in history; but in the sense that each myth must occupy a definite place in the whole system as a result of the fact that it is known to us in a cer-tain literary or pre-literary form. If one has probed the whole method of Lévi-Strauss and found it wanting, one can make a viable new start by seizing on the one aspect of mythology which he has neglected. If one makes this aspect one's central preoccupation, one may come up with the desired result, that is, with an interpretation of myth which makes use of no other principles than the ones which are inherent in mythology itself.

If one chooses the fact that there are different levels of oral or literary treatment as one's starting point, one must order myths according to their themes. One must sort all the myths in which a hero is wandering through the world and undergoes a series of trials or the myths in which a hero is sacrificed for the attainment of a greater good, and so forth. In order to arrange myths in series according to themes, one can choose them from different cultures and traditions and one will also be compelled to break up some stories into their episodic components even though they have been treated as a whole for centuries and possibly for millennia. One will search for the earliest tales and add to them more literate treatments and end up with the most sophisticated version undertaken for purely literary purposes. If one sorts myths in this fashion, one will make a striking discovery. One will discover that the various treatments of the same theme vary in specification of detail as well as in specification of plot. After much sorting and shuffling and analysis, one will be able to arrange each theme in a series in which the most general and unspecific treatment is at the bottom and the most specific treatment at the top.

The fact that one is able to arrange myths in typological series is of the utmost importance. It follows directly from two circumstances. First, myths have a history; and second, myths are not generated or created fully fledged but are gradually elaborated from simple, general tales into progressively more and more specific tales. The search for the earliest version is therefore never a search for the myth in its original most perfect and fully fledged form. Nor is it a search for the uncorrupted version. It is rather a search for the type, for the most unspecific version. The later versions, progressively specified, are the anti-types. Thus the very fact that myths have a historical dimension is responsible for the emergence of the typological series. Any attempt to interpret myths in terms of their original intentions, as Percy S. Cohen in his 1969 Malinowski Memorial Lecture[4] has done, is therefore basically misconceived because it fails to take account of the historical dimension and of the typological series which emerges as a result of this dimension, and starts with the search for the original intention as formulated in the earliest, fully fledged version. If one thinks one has found that first intention in the original version of the tale, one is also bound to consider all later versions of the story as so many corruptions. In short, the very idea that there is a golden age of myth and that all later versions are departures from and corruptions of the original version, is not only imaginary but also flies in the face of all the evidence. For the evidence shows us without the slightest shadow of a doubt that myths have histories; that we know of myths only in their historical dimension and that no one version of any tale as it has come down to us, whatever the method of tradition, is more 'original' or more 'true' than any other version.

Examples are not difficult to find and Alister Cameron[5] has described the different literary versions of the Oedipus myth and shown how there is a progress towards specification – so much so that the last, most specified version of Sophocles comes very near to a conceptual statement. In the *Iliad* there is a brief reference to the tale in which Oedipus is a warrior, killed in battle and buried with traditional funeral honours. In the *Odyssey*, the story is enlarged: Oedipus continues to rule after the death of Jocasta, in spite of the fact that the Gods had revealed to him that he had married his mother and killed his father. In another epic version, the *Thebais*, there is no incest, for Oedipus begets his children with Euryganeia. The children are under a curse – but Oedipus's role in the tragedy is minimal. In Aeschylus's treatment, the story is blown up into a regular tragedy. Jocasta appears as Oedipus's wife and the incest is fully established, and so is the parricide which takes place at a crossroads in Potniae, situated on the road from Thebes to Platea. Although the Delphic oracle is mentioned, it plays a minor part, for it is an oracle given to Laius. Moreover, Potniae means the 'place of the dread Goddesses', that is the Furies. And thus the whole tragedy is centred upon the Furies, who become the agents of the hereditary curse working through three generations. The story is one of crime and retribution and the role of the Furies is the binding, formal principle of the story. In this sense, the myth is similar to the story of Orestes as told by Aeschylus and does not by itself exhibit any specific features.

With Sophocles, we come to a more highly specific version.

Sophocles eliminates the central role of the Furies and plays down the theme of crime and retribution. Instead he moves Delphi into the centre of the story. First, by making the parricide take place near Daulis in the Phocian Pass on the road from Thebes to Delphi. The fateful meeting of father and son takes place as the oracle is being consulted. Second, Sophocles introduces a second oracle, given to Oedipus, so that Oedipus knows that he will kill his father and marry his mother. And with Delphi, Apollo, the God of light and self-knowledge, moves into the foreground. And finally, Sophocles gives further specification in harmony with the Apollo theme. Oedipus, in the end, discovers his own identity as the son of his wife and the murderer of his father. In this way the discovery becomes self-discovery and self-knowledge in obedience to the Delphic Apollo.

The typological seriality of the Oedipus story, from modest beginnings to the grand finale of an almost conceptual summary in Sophocles, is an example in a very circumscribed time-span. Whatever the antecedents, from Homer's first formulation to Sophocles there elapsed no more than three or four centuries and the development of the tale all took place in a single cultural environment.

On a much wider canvas, Fontenrose[6] has established the typological seriality of a large number of combat myths. He distinguishes three different ranges of specificity. There is first the long distance range, the myths of combat distributed over much of ancient Asia and Europe. Then there is the middle distance range, which contains the story of Apollo's combat with the dragon in the Homeric hymn to Apollo as well as the many other versions that are to be found in Euripides and Ovid, Simonides and Lucian. In the same middle distance range, there is the version in which the combat takes place between Zeus and Typhon. In these versions of the middle distance range, Fontenrose points out, the champion god is opposing a not completely specified opponent. The opponent is sometimes male, sometimes female. And when female, she appears sometimes as a seductress or temptress figure who lures the hero to his (temporary) doom, and here we have the Venusberg theme. Alternately, she may sometimes appear as the champion's wife or sister and lure the enemy to (temporary) destruction – and here we have the Judith and Holofernes theme. Finally we come across the near range versions of combat, told with a much higher degree of specificity, about such heroes as Perseus and Heracles. Wisely and perceptively Fontenrose concludes his long survey and analysis of this material with the remark that 'we may look upon the whole combat in all its forms as the conflict between Eros and Thanatos. It is that opposition between life instincts and death instincts that Freud was the first to formulate, albeit tentatively, as the central principle of all living organisms from the beginning.' Although Fontenrose does not spell it out, he clearly points the lesson.[7] Freud's formula comes as the last step in the typological chain – yet another version of the old theme; but this time so highly specified that it appears in the shape of a conceptual formula rather than as yet another tale. In passing we might anticipate a little of the argument to follow. The observation of living organisms would never have enabled Freud to formulate his famous theory. The theory was clearly suggested to him by his knowledge of the mythological series. He was thus able to arrive at a great insight about nature through his knowledge of mythology. His mere observation of nature would never have yielded the precise data for the theory about life and death instinct; for the mere data to be gathered from natural observation would have suggested, and indeed have suggested to other observers, other theories. But, and this final comment is crucial, having formulated his abstract theory on the basis of his knowledge of a long mythical typology, he was then able to turn round and interpret nature in the light of this theory and find, amid the vast mass of evidence offered by nature, much evidence to support the theory and many processes on which the theory could shed a new light.

One can watch another example of typological seriality on an even vaster scale, stretching over more than a millennium and developing in a variety of cultural environments. The example I have in mind is the story of creation.[8] Here again, the earliest forms are unknown to us although it is not very difficult to imagine the type of natural event of which the first mythical image is a transformation. The first semi-literary treatment is to be found among the Sumerians. The goddess Nammu (probably synonymous with the sea), so the story goes, gave birth to heaven and earth. And then the High God Enlil raped the goddess Ninlil and thus, after many vicissitudes, the various parts of the universe were born. Finally the gods created man out of clay because they were tired of having to work for their living and preferred the ground to be tilled by man and man to serve them. In Babylonia, the story took a different form. Marduk, the myth goes, conquered Tiamat. Thus he secured the tablets of destiny and then created the world. Marduk was the progeny of Enki, the god of wisdom and magic. There is no need to recite the details of the struggle between Marduk and Tiamat. Marduk's final enthronement as king and his organisation of the universe, however, make it quite clear that the creation of the world had something to do with the struggle of moral forces and we may take it that as against the Sumerian version, we have here a typological specification. As against the Sumerian version, the Babylonian version is more specific in that it attributes a master's, not to say creator's role to a male deity. The variations on the theme in Ugarit and among the Hittites have been traced by scholars. Eventually a birfurcation took place and during the seventh and eighth centuries B.C. there appear two further specified, parallel versions, one in the Old Testament, and the other by Hesiod. In the Old Testament stories (Genesis 1–2:4a and 2:4b–25) God is said to have been the creator of the universe out of watery chaos or out of waterless waste. He then created animals, plants and men and laid down a moral law. We have here a very high degree of specification even though the type of the story is clearly discernible. In Hesiod, the type is even more clearly discernible and we owe it to the researches of Cornford that the typological seriality between the ancient Sumerian and Babylonian myths and the myth of Hesiod is clearly established. It has since been greatly strengthened by the publication of the fragments of the Hittite–Hurrian *Epic of Kumarbi*. The Hurrian tale of wars in Heaven was taken over by the Hittites, from whom it found its way to the Greeks. But whatever the methods of culture contact and diffusion, the important point is the progressive specification which reached its climax in Hesiod's version.[9] First there was chaos, and next, earth. Chaos gave birth to Night and Erebus; and the union of Night with Erebus produced Bright Sky and Day, and so forth until we come to the drama of Zeus, the battle of the gods and the creation of animals and men. In Hesiod, the story reaches a semi-philosophical abstraction. It is so highly specified that, as Cornford[10] has plausibly argued, there was only a small step required to make the transition from Hesiod's myth to Anaximander's cosmogony. Cornford has taken special pains to show how Anaximander's concept of *apeiron* could not have been formed on the basis of natural evidence and must therefore be considered as a conceptualisation of a mythical image.

By the same process, as is well known, the creation story of the Old Testament was eventually conceptualised and transformed into a philosophical cosmogony in the middle ages when it was systematised, with the help of Aristotelian concepts, by St Thomas Aquinas, and turned into the theology of creation *ex nihilo*. Perhaps the intermediary step of St John's formulation that 'in the beginning there was the *logos*' played an important role, and helped St Thomas to arrive at his conceptualisation. However this may be, both St Thomas and Anaximander provided a theoretical, conceptual antitype to an earlier non-specific type.[11]

The importance of Cornford's theory cannot be exaggerated.[12] He clearly demonstrated the existence of the long series which stretches from ancient Sumer to Hesiod and found its final conceptualisation in Anaximander. Although he himself did not investigate the parallel development among the Hebrews and Christians which led to St Thomas Aquinas, the fact that this parallel development took place enhances the importance of Cornford's discovery. It was perhaps unfortunate that Cornford himself was less interested in the typological seriality of these stories than in the theory that myth is based on ritual. Many of his sympathetic critics and all his detractors have therefore paid little attention to the real importance of his discovery and confined themselves instead to pointing out that the theory of the ritual foundations of mythology stands on very shaky grounds. It is quite irrelevant for the purposes of the present argument whether Cornford is right in his contention that myth is based on ritual or not. The real importance of Cornford's book consists in the demonstration to which he himself did not pay much attention, that there was typological seriality.

FIVE

THE OPPORTUNISM
OF STRUCTURALISM

Before proceeding with the argument, it is as well to pause and consider that it is possible to break these vast typological series up and to take each version by itself in relation to the social order which produced it. We have been furnished with a detailed structural analysis of the Biblical creation myth by Leach.[1] The story, when subdivided, consists of three repetitive messages. The first is the creation of the world; the second, the story of the Garden of Eden; and the third, the tale of Cain and Abel. In each story, he showed, there is a conflict between death and life, God and man. In each story the static or dead world is made 'alive' or moving by the agency of a factor which mediates between the two opposite poles.

It is equally possible to provide a structural analysis of Hesiod's *Theogony*.[2] Indeed, a structural analysis will reveal a formal perfection by comparison with which the structure of the Biblical creation myth is confused.

Hesiod's story can be broken up into eight episodes:

1. Earth and Heaven, in sexual union, produce Oceanus and Rhea (water and earth) and other deities.
2. Erebus and Night, in sexual union, produce Aether and Day.
3. Cronos castrates Ouranos, his father, and uses the genitals as seeds.
4. Zeus vanquishes Cronos, his father, and frees the children which Cronos had devoured.
5. Earth brings forth Heaven and Pontus, the infertile sea.
6. Chaos brings forth Erebus and Night.
7. Ouranos prevents the children he has fathered from leaving their mother's (Earth) womb.

8. Cronos devours the children whom Rhea (Cybele, Magna Mater, Earth) has borne.

First of all, episodes 1–4 are stories of fertility. In 1 and 2, there is a sexual union which is blessed with offspring. In 3 and 4, there is release, brought about in 3 by castration and in 4 by simple vanquishing of the agent of infertility. All stories state that there is multiplication. In the first two, multiplication is due to sexual union; in the second two, to cutting something off and to releasing something. Furthermore, each pair of multiplication stories consists of opposites. For the first pair of stories are stories of incestuous union, for according to 5 Earth is the mother of Heaven; and according to 7, Erebus is the sibling of Night. Story 1 is a tale of incest between mother and son, and story 2 a tale of incest between brother and sister. The second pair of multiplication stories are similarly opposite to one another. Both are stories in which the son overcomes the father. But in 3, multiplication is due to the use of the genitals as seeds; and in story 4, multiplication is due to the fact that the children imprisoned in Cronos are let out. Furthermore, there is an opposition in the roles of Cronos and Ouranos. Cronos, by eating his children, imitates a womb, that is, the male tries to be female. Ouranos, on the other side, by not allowing his spouse to give birth to the children she has conceived, exaggeratedly plays the dominating male who refuses to let the female be female. By contrast, Ouranos, the exaggerated male, is castrated and his severed genitals are used as seeds. The exaggerated male figure of Ouranos is thus turned into seeds. Cronos, on the other hand, imitates femininity by trying to be a womb to his children. When his son Zeus vanquishes him, the children he has eaten are freed and rise as if Cronos had been a womb to them. Ouranos, who tried to deny femininity, is destroyed and his genitals are used as seeds, that is, he is forcibly reminded that he is male. Cronos, who tried to imitate femininity, is destroyed and forcibly reminded that if he wishes to pretend to be a womb, he must act like one. It then appears that in 3 and 4 the sons actually play along with their fathers' aspirations and pretensions. In 3, Ouranos's exaggerated maleness of 7 is accepted by his son: Cronos plays along with it and uses his blood or genitals as semen, thus merely cutting Ouranos's aspirations down to size, i.e. he makes him into an ordinary male. In 4, Zeus 'vanquishes' (rapes?)

Cronos – Zeus plays along with Cronos's exaggerated femininity of story 8. He treats him like a woman and 'vanquishes' him, thus making him into an ordinary woman who is fertile.

Next, let us consider the second set of stories, 5–8. These stories are all stories of infertility. Story 5 tells that Earth produced Heaven and the infertile Sea. Story 6 tells that Chaos produced Erebus (Darkness) and Night. Story 7 tells us that Ouranos entombed his children in their mother's womb and story 8 tells us that Cronos devoured his children, i.e. entombed them in himself. Here again, we have two sets of opposites. Stories 5 and 6 are stories about some form of parthenogenesis: Earth, unaided, produces Heaven and Sea – Chaos, unaided, produces Erebus and Night. The result is some form of sterility. The second pair, stories 7 and 8, are entombment stories. In story 7, Ouranos refuses to let his children be born and turns their mother's womb into their tomb; and in story 8, Cronos devours his children and thus turns himself into their tomb. And finally, to make the symmetry of oppositions complete, there is an opposition between 5 and 6; and between 7 and 8. In story 5, Earth is derivative ('next wide-blossomed Earth came to be . . .'). In story 6, Chaos, whatever that is, is primary ('Verily, at first Chaos came to be . . .'). A similar opposition is to be found between stories 7 and 8. In story 7, Ouranos entombs his children in their mother and in story 8, Cronos turns himself into his children's tomb. This means that Ouranos exaggerates masculinity by dominating his spouse; and Cronos femininity, by imitating his spouse.

Finally, to crown the edifice, we find that the second set of events, the stories of infertility, are turned into stories of fertility or made into stories with a – happy – fertile, ending. Stories 5 and 6 receive their happy, fertile ending by being followed up with stories 1 and 2 respectively. Earth's and Chaos's parthenogenesis was infertile. But their sterile offspring (Heaven and infertile Sea; Erebus and Night) are made to have incestuous sexual intercourse. And incest, as opposed to parthenogenesis, has non-steril results. In story 1 mother–son incest produces the fertile oceans and Rhea–Cybele and others. In story 2, brother–sister incest produces the light of day (Aether) and Day. Similarly, stories 7 and 8 are provided with a happy, fertile ending by stories 3 and 4. Ouranos's attempt at entombment of his children is frustrated by the efforts of his son Cronos and thus story 7, originally a story of sterility, is turned, by story 3, into a story of fertility. Cronos's attempt to prevent fertility by devouring his children is frustrated by his son Zeus and thus story 8 ends as a story of fertility when linked with story 4, in which Zeus frees the children entombed in Cronos.

The structural parallelism and the artful oppositions in Hesiod are masterly. They show us that there was exaggerated fertility and exaggerated sterility and that, when the second set of stories are linked with the first set of stories, that is when there is mediation between too much fertility and too much sterility, a balance is brought about – a balance which is in fact the orderly disposition of the universe and the world of man.

The structural analyses of both the Biblical and the Hesiodic creation myths are wholly convincing. The question which we are, however, forced to ask, is: so what? The authors of the Biblical creation myth and Hesiod are by no means the only artists of structural involution and opposition, conversion and inversion. It is one of the fundamental laws of aesthetics that an artistically presented story should be capable of such structural analysis. The history of literature is full of examples. Choosing examples at random, we need only remind ourselves of the masterly structuralism of Proust or of Ibsen's *Hedda Gabler*. Proust, indeed, provides the full structural analysis of *A la Recherche du temps perdu* on the last pages of the last volume. 'I saw Gilberte coming towards me ... was (her daughter) not like the centre of crossroads in a forest, the point where roads converge from many directions?'[3] Proust then goes on to describe that in Gilberte's daughter all the movements of his experiences met in one single point. Through her father, she belonged to the Guermantes way and through her mother, to Swann's way. Swann was the commoner who wanted to rise in the social scale. The Guermantes were the aristocrats who had started to marry beneath themselves. Moreover, Swann had married Odette, whom Proust had first met in very doubtful circumstances which eventually led him to the even more doubtful circumstances of the homosexuality practised by some of the Guermantes. There is no need to pursue the matter in detail. But Proust was aware that Swann's way exaggerated the importance of nobility, and the Guermantes's way, the precariousness of nobility; and how, through a family of footmen, common to both ways, Swann and the Guermantes had been brought together, but that these footmen were precisely the agents of sexual inversion

35

D

– so that sexual inversion runs parallel to the social inversion manifest in Swann's daughter's rise and the Duchess de Guermantes's descent. To crown it all, Vinteuil's music, an obvious moment of great aesthetic beauty, plays a role of 'bringing together' which is completely analogous to the role of homosexuality. The mixing of the two sides (Méséglise and Guermantes) is brought about by homosexuality (the homosexual footman's uncle is the gent who reveals the true identity of Odette); and by Vinteuil's music. Both agents of mixture (low and high) are combined in the story of the Lesbian Mlle Vinteuil who spits on her father's picture as she seduces her girlfriend – and this theme is *inverted* in Gilberte's daughter who is *not* a snob and marries beneath her. She too, like Mlle Vinteuil, perversely offends her parents. She has the right motive and it is her offended mother who is silly, whereas Mlle Vinteuil had the wrong motive (pleasure and evil) and her offended father is good (author of the music). On p.413, Proust even provides the theory of structural analysis by reminding his readers that such analysis was made possible by the fact that memory, 'by introducing the past into the present without modification, as though it were the present, eliminates precisely the great Time-dimension in accordance with which life is realised'. This passage anticipates the assumptions of Lévi-Strauss's structuralism word for word and could easily have been quoted by him. The only difference between Proust and Lévi-Strauss here is that Proust's statement is preceded by a lengthy description of the psychological experience of the disappearance of time. Hence his justification of a structural analysis in which the whole of his life appears as a structured set of contemporary events. What Proust tells us is, precisely, that on the premise that 'time is regained', our experiences do not present themselves as a random collection but as a structural collection and that it requires an artist's talent and work to analyse the structure. Proust's well-known insistence on the importance of the artist's contribution for the revelation of structure underlines the present argument. For the present argument contends that any particular myth which exhibits structure is a more or less artful and artistic construct accomplished by a certain known or unknown person at a particular moment in history and can be typologically related to other such constructs; but cannot be equated without more ado with mythology as such and considered the precipitate of the human mind manifest in a given social order. In

Lévi-Strauss, on the other hand, there is no claim to a personal psychological experience which erases time; but merely an attempt to explain the relationship between myths and societies as if the time dimension did not exist. We can approve of Proust, because the matter presents itself as a personal aesthetic consciousness. We can not, on the same grounds, approve of Lévi-Strauss. Or take Ibsen. In *Hedda Gabler* there is an opposition between life and death, represented by Hedda and Lovborg on the side of creative life; and Tesman and Mrs Elvsted, on the other side. At the beginning of the play, they are ill-matched in opposites, that is Hedda and Tesman and Lovborg and Mrs Elvsted. The ensuing drama is made up of the sorting out of these ill-matched couples, so that the play ends with Hedda and Lovborg on one side, and Tesman and Mrs Elvsted on the other. But, it turns out, the two life forces are dead; and the two death forces are alive. Moreover, Hedda and Lovborg present life in its opposite poles. Hedda is exaggerated sterility, i.e. a woman trying to imitate a man, a woman without children, a woman who burns the literary creations of another man. Lovborg, at the opposite pole, is exaggerated creativity; i.e. he is drunk, his visions are utopian and he commits suicide when he loses his manuscripts. Hedda and Lovborg could have come together creatively had they been able to tone down these exaggerations. As it is, their contact turned life into death. But all this is neither here nor there, for the possibility of structural analysis, as I have argued above, is not disputed.[4] What is disputed is the contention that such structural analysis transcends the functioning of a myth in a specific social setting and if anything, Leach's structural analysis of Genesis confirms precisely that structurally, a myth such as the Biblical creation story can be seen as a message or series of messages making life tolerable to people who are plagued by the thought that incest is prohibited and yet necessary; that life and death are opposed and yet due to the same God, and so on.

SIX

TYPOLOGICAL
INTERPRETATION

Granting the possibility of structural analysis, one should still not blind oneself to the fact that myths have historical dimensions; that in their historical dimensions they appear as typological series proceeding, as time goes by, towards higher degrees of specification. The real crux of the matter, then, is not whether myths should be interpreted structurally or functionally; but that apart from being capable of being interpreted functionally in a structural manner, they can also be seen as arranged in long typological series, completely divorced from the social order in which any one link of the typological chain happens to have been composed.

But there is a historical consideration which throws much doubt on the relevance of a structural analysis of, say, Hesiod and the Biblical creation myth. The structural analysis throws much light on the aesthetics of Ibsen and Proust. But where do we go from here? We know very little about the society in which the authors of the Biblical creation myth lived and not much more about the society in which Hesiod lived. Must we assume that these authors wrote their myths in order to resolve certain doubts as to the opposition between life and death or the opposition between sterility and fertility among their fellow-citizens? If these myths are taken to make life tolerable by removing incomprehensible and therefore intolerable oppositions, ought we not then to wonder as to the precise form in which these myths were *popularly* current? All we have, for purposes of structural analysis, are the highly literary forms of these myths. In other words, we do not have these myths in the shape in which they fulfilled a 'function' in certain societies; but only in a definite literary shape. And, what is more, we cannot maintain that the structural analysis is valid for any of their historical precursors or popular prototypes. For the structure, as revealed in the analyses presented, is strictly an analysis of the structure of these stories in a *definite and unique form.* We cannot even combine structural analysis with the typological series; for we have no reason to think that the structure of Hesiod's version is reflective and can be found in any of the typological antecedents. Let us consider, on an even grander scale, myths of sacrifice. They can be arranged in such a way that at the bottom of the series there is a story in which there is a sacrifice, but no indication as to who is being sacrificed to whom by whom and for what purpose:

> 'I knew that I hung on the wind-swept tree
> Nine nights through,
> Wounded by a spear, dedicated to Odin,
> I myself to myself.'

Next comes a version in which one or more of these features is made more specific, and so forth, until, at the top of a series, we have the same theme treated very specifically as, say, the sacrifice of the Son of God by God for the sake of redemption. The increase in specification need not necessarily correspond to the succession of these treatments of the theme in time. There is no absolute necessity why a general and unspecified version should be an earlier one although, as a matter of experience, one will frequently find that the more unspecified version is in fact the earlier version.

If one, next, looks at the bottom of the series, one will find that it diverges only in small details, if at all, from a rational event or occurrence.

The first mythical formulation is often very modest and shows almost no signs of extravagance or supernatural complexity. There are tribes and castes in India whose tales concern nothing more intricate than a being consisting of two crossed sticks and the ancient Romans observed a worshipful attitude to nothing more non-natural than the hearth fire, an event so ordinary that they did not even think it worthwhile to *tell* a tale about it.

A highly unspecific treatment of the sacrifice theme may state no more than that a certain animal was slaughtered. In this unspecified form, the tale is barely different from a natural occurrence which everybody can watch every day. In this form, it is wide open. Nevertheless, there will be a formalism, a repetitiveness, an emphasis which will make it different from a report of a natural event and thus clearly single it out as a myth. In fact, the very earliest or unspecific version of the myth differs from a recital of a natural event only in formal details. It diverges from a report of a natural event or occurrence, perhaps, only because some slightly incredible feature has been introduced; and at times, when an incredible feature is lacking, it may differ from a report of a natural occurrence by nothing more than the opening line, 'Once upon a time . . .', which indicates that it is remembered although, unlike natural occurrences, it cannot be located to have taken place at any one particular or precise point in time.

This observation draws our attention to the fact that in its (earliest?) unspecified form, there is only a very slight, perhaps imperceptible transition, a very slight difference between a myth and a report of a natural event. And, for the sake of completeness, we ought, therefore, to add a special bottom to our series. This rock-bottom consists of a report of the natural event from which the first story in our series is the initial divergence.

Unfortunately students of myth usually neglect the initial stage of transition from a purely natural event to the earliest, unspecified mythical tale. If I suggest that the earliest stage, in which a natural story or a historical event is deflected into a myth and embroidered accordingly, is worthy of consideration, I do not mean that it is important to start with a historical inquiry into the origins of any myth. Such an inquiry must always be condemned to failure because the historical origins are shrouded in complete darkness. As against this, an inquiry into the logical connection between a historical event or a natural event and the first slight deflection into myth is important and fruitful, because it shows us that every mythical series has its origins in natural material, embroidered and organised for the sake of emphasis and clarity. If we have a mythical series about a giant, there is no point in inquiring who the historical prototype of the giant actually was. But it is important to understand that the image of the giant is due to a deflection of or embroidery of a story about a human being of extraordinary size. The initial stage of transition from a natural event to a mythical tale is also important because it reminds us that the supernatural and extraordinary elements in myth are the result of this deflection, not the other way round. Many people have believed that men first sense the Holy[1] or the Supernatural and then invent or create myths to do justice to their intuition. If we keep our eyes firmly on the first step in the mythical series, we will recognise that the reverse is the case. The notion of the Supernatural is an extrapolation or abstraction from the myth and its first shadow was introduced in the first stage in which a natural event is deflected into an as yet unspecific myth. This consideration has also some bearing upon the relationship between history and myth. In many cases in which the beginnings of the series are not shrouded in complete darkness – the Old Testament is full of such cases – we can actually detect how a historical occurrence is mythologised. People take an old ritual and assimilate a historical event to it. The origins of the Feasts of Tabernacles and of Passover are cases in point. Nature festivals were historicised and then the historicisation, in turn, gave rise to a myth or, more precisely to mythicised history. Such mythologisation of a historical event is rarely the beginning of the series; but it represents a powerful new stage in the development of the series. The new development stems from the fact that the series is typologically specified not by a further nature myth, i.e. by an elaboration of a natural event, but by the elaboration of a historical event. In his contribution to *Before Philosophy*[2] H. Frankfort called this process the 'emancipation of thought from myth'. But it would have been more appropriate to describe it as the transformation of nature myth into historical myth – for the description of the exodus from Egypt is not presented as a cold-blooded historical narrative but as a myth the several ingredients of which are both historical events and natural events, the latter having already undergone ritual specification and the former being assimilated to the latter.

Historical events, like the events of nature (birth, death, the seasons, marriage, etc.) can be elaborated typologically. But since historical events are usually remembered with a time-index of some kind or other, unlike natural events, they rarely form the *beginning* of a series as they stand. In most cases they are intruded into an already existing one. They are first mythicised or assimilated to an already existing myth or ritual and then elaborated further. It often looks as if the historical event (the foundation of Rome, the exodus from Egypt, the murder of Gessler by William Tell) is taken as it stands and used as the bottom of the series, pre-figuring other stories. But the appearance is deceptive. The historical event becomes part of the series only after it has been assimilated to a myth, of which, in its assimilated form, it then becomes an anti-type. As such it is intruded into the series. The role of ordinary historical events is therefore different from the part played by ordinary natural events. Both natural and historical events can be 'ordinary' in the same sense. But there is a difference between the ways in which they become part of typological series. But just as we find, behind a sacred marriage myth, an ordinary marriage, we often find, behind a mythicised historical event, a genuine historical kernel eventually discovered by archaeology.

This question deserves closer examination. We know of many cases in which plain historical events have become assimilated to a mythological series. In his *Thucydides Mythistoricus*, Cornford has provided a classic example of the assimilation of ordinary historical events – in this case of the Peloponnesian War – into a mythological pattern. We also know how Livy, basing himself on earlier traditions, took many events from very early Roman history and mythologised them not by turning history into mythology but by taking an ancient mythology and assimilating historical fact to it. Archaeologists have found much material during their excavations which relates to the story of Romulus and Remus and for this reason there is nothing fanciful in Momigliano's suggestion that the historical foundation of Rome bears much greater resemblance to the story told by Livy than most historians have been willing to admit. The natural, historical events were not the starting point of a myth but were recounted by Livy and his predecessors in a form assimilated to mythical tales. 'The Romans,' writes Michael Grant, 'were abnormally single-minded in this conversion of their mythology into history.' That is why there emerged this great hulk of fictitious history or para-history or higher truth relating to Rome, which only occasionally coincides with that other kind of truth that we learn about from the archaeologists.[3] Yet another example comes from the Old Testament. The ritual and myth of the Passover festival are much older than the historical exodus from Egypt. But the events immediately preceding the historical exodus were assimilated to the ritual and myth of Passover and eventually it was believed that Passover was celebrated in commemoration of these historical events preceding the exodus. Here we have instances of the absorption of ordinary, natural historical occurrences into mythological traditions.

We also know of cases where the opposite happened. We know that in some instances a plain historical occurrence was taken as the first natural occurrence and then became the type for the elaboration of mythical anti-types. The story of the resurrection of Jesus Christ is a case in point and will be considered at greater length below. At the same time it is worth remembering that the mythologisation of historical events, in which historical events become the starting point of a mythological series, is comparatively rare. The opposite development, in which a historical occurrence is assimilated to an already current mythical series, is much more common. For that matter, it is debatable whether the story of the resurrection of Jesus Christ is really an example of the mythologisation of a historical event or an example of the assimilation of a historical event to a pre-existing mythical pattern. For, supposing the resurrection was a historical event, it is clear that, whatever subsequent embroidery did to it, the historical event such as it was, was assimilated to the long tradition of stories about gods who die and are resurrected.

If one is concerned with the development of mythical elaboration and embroidery, the question of the role of historical events is not all that important. At best, it represents a special instance of the general role played by perfectly natural events in the formation of mythical tales. Every natural event, the slaughter of a sheep or the birth of a baby, is historical in the sense that it must take place at a certain time and a certain place. Mythical elaboration of the natural event is usually fairly uninterested in the precise historical location of the natural event it makes use of, and any historical connotation of time and place is soon forgotten because it is considered irrelevant. Nevertheless, it is worth pointing out that datable historical occurrences, like undatable actual occurrences such as thunderstorms and cloudbursts, births of babies and slaughters of rams, do play a detectable part in the evolution of mythical typological series.

In fact, often the first stage of deflection is a mere prising loose of an event from its position in time and space and an addition of the formula 'Once upon a time . . .' as an introduction to the story which relates the event. This first deflection from natural and literal truth is very easily achieved because most primitive people have no time-reckoning system related to an absolutely fixed point such as the birth of Christ or the foundation of the city of Rome. It is therefore very easy for them to create myth from nature by simply losing track of the precise point in time and space at which a story happened and thus make it carry, by prising it loose and depriving it of its status of a particular event, a meaning over and above the meaning the particular event had at the time and the place at which it occurred. The story that a baby was born at a certain time and place has a particular meaning and nothing else. But if the story is prefaced by the formula 'Once upon a time a baby was born ...' it immediately assumes a higher level of meaningfulness, even when there is no other elaboration. It is worth noting that the exact location in time, because of the widespread absence of time-reckoning systems, is much more frequently lost sight of than the exact location in space at which a mythical event has occurred. The world is full of spots, trees, hills, caves, etc., at which events said to be mythical have taken place. But it is of the essence of myth, in many cases, that the location in time is omitted. We can therefore safely conclude that a natural occurrence can easily be turned into myth without any further elaboration by depriving it of its connection with a location in time; but that further elaboration is needed when it is not deprived of its location in time and that deprivation of its connection with a certain time is much more common than deprivation of its connection with a certain space. Places can be remembered more easily than locations in time and it is very rare for the first deflection of nature into myth to consist of nothing but a prising loose of an event in nature from the location in space in which it has occurred. But it is very common for the first deflection of nature into myth to consist of nothing more elaborate than the omission of its location in time.

There is yet another reason for bearing the initial stage of the deflection of a natural event into a mythical tale in mind. Ever since men have started to reflect on the meaning of myth, they have been troubled by the anthropomorphic character of most mythical tales. Sceptics have always believed that their detection of human and natural features in almost all myths is a sign of their untrustworthiness. But if one bears in mind the first initial stage in which the natural and human raw material we find in every-day experience, sex, slaughter, battles, contests, etc., are mythically embroidered – tentatively at first and in a rather unspecific manner – it cannot be a great surprise to find that even in its very last stages of high specificity and precision, a myth should retain parts of the raw

material. The human imagination, after all, is limited. It can specify
and make more precise by breaking the natural ingredients up and
re-assembling them in a new manner. But it can never transcend
the raw elements taken from our natural experience and eliminate them from myth. We can imagine gods that are immortal; but we
cannot imagine gods that are totally different from beings we know.
We can transpose the head of an elephant to a trunk of a human
being, and vice versa. We can make fish walk and women fly by giving them the wings of birds. But the imagination will not carry us
beyond such images. Nor need such an admission force us to yield
to the sceptic and dismiss myths as untrustworthy fantasy. For if
we remember the growing development towards greater specification,
if we remember that myths come in progressive series, the revelatory
element of myths must be sought in the progress towards precision
of the image, rather than in the non-anthropomorphic character of
the raw material that is used in the stories.

Finally, the importance of the first stage of deflection is often
appreciated but misinterpreted. The history of the interpretation of
mythology is full of attempts to prove that the first stage, the deflection from a natural occurrence to a mythical tale, took place but that
it ought not to have taken place. The mythical tale is not considered, as it ought to be, as the first tentative and fumbling attempt
to break away from the unembroidered statement of natural fact in
order to convey something over and above it; but is considered as a
substitution of a mythical (i.e. false) tale or image for a natural fact.
These interpretations of mythology as substitutions of something
unreal or visionary for something true and given and natural range
from the nineteenth-century attempts to see myths as substitutes
for stars or the moon or the sun to modern sociologising variations
according to which myths are substitutions for certain types of social
order and tales about spiritual beings are conceptualisations of the
constitutional structures of social life. It seems that these substitution interpretations, though not wrong, are a blind alley, for they
misunderstand the substitution as a final product and do not treat
it as the first step in an ascending and developing series.

Having thus added to our series of myths, ordered according to
the degree of specification with which the myth is told, a further
bottom, we turn to the top of the series. There we can frequently
observe that the degree of specification is unusually high. We may

not only find that it is spelt out who is being sacrificed to whom and for what reason; but also, that the sacrificer and the sacrificed being are circumstantially defined as entities or beings of whom we have no direct knowledge or experience. They may be conceptually defined as the Son of God and as God Himself, triune, omnipotent and omniscient. In other words, at the top of the series, we will find a version of the theme which is not only specific but contains all the ingredients for a translation of the story into a conceptual definition. We must, therefore, make an addition to the top of our series and add, as the last layer, the conceptual definition of the story. In this last layer we will not have a story telling us that something concrete happened; but an abstract theory to the effect that the Trinity sacrificed itself in order to redeem the world it had created. This theory – for we are now clearly in the realm of theory and no longer in the realm of mythical tales – can be further transformed into more abstract speculation to the effect that the World turns back upon itself in order to continue the incessant creation of itself by itself.

If the bottom and the top layer are thus added to the series, we can learn something about its inherent meaning. We first of all watch the direction in which the first divergence from a report of a natural event to a myth takes place. Then we gauge, by following the stages of progressive specification, the sense of direction. And finally, we can discover how the whole series is topped off not by a further story but by a conceptual summing up of the whole series. In such a series, we call the earlier story a type of a later story; or we can say that an earlier, less specified story pre-figured the later story. The whole series, especially if one takes the additional bottom layer and the additional top layer into consideration, becomes a typological system.

One of the most striking and complete instances of such a typological system stretching from a ritual-myth barely distinguishable from a natural event to a highly conceptualised metaphysical system is provided in Indian thought. It is perhaps the only case where the whole series from the bottom layer to the top layer can be fully documented.[4] Starting at the end of nature with a communal repast, we find that it was ritualised and provided with a minimum specification in the *Rg Veda*. From there we go to the *Brāhmanas*, to those hymns in which the science of sacrifice is elaborated, and from there we pass to the *Upanishads* which bring us through further specifications to the threshold of metaphysical abstraction. The next step is represented by the *Brāhma Sutra*, a collection of aphoristic summaries of the *Upanishads*. The final point of conceptualisation was reached when Sankara wrote his commentary on the *Brāhma Sutra*. Although his writings contain frequent traces of purely logical reasoning, he himself was under no illusion as to what precisely he was doing when he presented his metaphysics of *Advaita Vedanta*. He offered it as a commentary on the *Brāhma Sutra*, that is, as a final specification of the meaning of the aphorisms. All these steps in the series are extant and provide therefore a fully documented example of the transformation of nature into myth, the specification of myth into highly detailed symbols and aphorisms and, finally, the transformation of the aphorisms into metaphysical concepts. The communal repast is the type; Sankara's metaphysics, the anti-type.

The existence of typological relationships was observed first by writers in early Christian times. It enabled them to explain the relationship between the stories of the Old Testament and the New Testament and, in some cases, between pagan myths and Christian stories. They used to say that the older myths prefigured the later ones or that the older ones were the types of the later ones. The later myths were called the anti-types. The appropriateness of the observation that myths came in typological series cannot be doubted. The observation, as one can imagine, was however put to a very limited use. It was used to demonstrate that there is some kind of divine providence which reveals truths gradually and thus it was believed that the type stands to the anti-type in a relationship which was described as exemplary causality. I am not here suggesting that we revive the notion of exemplary causality. But the phenomenon which gave rise to the notion is real enough.

The important consideration is that one can learn very little, if anything, from merely surveying any two layers of the series. One can call them the type and anti-type and maintain that the one prefigured the other. But one will be none the wiser for it. One can only gauge the inherent meaning of the theme by watching the whole of the series, or, at least, a very large part of it. If one thus makes use of the natural or historical fact that myths have come down to us in varying degrees of specification, one can eventually hope to determine the meaning of any one theme of mythology. One can say that the theme 'means' the last and most highly specified conceptual formulation.

First, we must note that no ultimate conceptual formulation is possible unless the whole or a very large part of the series is taken into account. Since there is progressive specification over the whole series, starting with a tale which is nothing but a report of a natural event, it is impossible to transform any single layer of the series into a conceptual formula. If one tried, one would be guilty of arbitrary transformation; for there would be no telling which way the transformation would go. One has to gauge the sense of direction from the whole series by watching which elements are being specified further in each layer and how they are being specified in order to be able to make the final transformation in line with the whole series.

Second, we must note that in this method of interpretation, which is obviously completely non-functional, there is no question of translation or of decoding. The myths are not taken as a language which conveys a message; but as ends in themselves. They are entities which reveal their meaning because they appear, as a matter of history, in series of progressive specification. Instead of our translating them into other languages, they yield up their meaning of their own accord because they further and further specify themselves until they are so specific that the transformation into a conceptual sentence is almost imperceptible. It is, indeed, often difficult to tell where myth ends and conceptual theory begins.

Third, it now becomes apparent that the bottom layer, the natural event, pre-figures the ultimate conceptually expressed theory. It is the type; and the theory is the anti-type. The important thing to notice here is that one could, however, never proceed straight from the original type to the ultimate anti-type. Who could possibly guess, when hearing a report of a killing of an animal, that it *means* the self-destruction of the creative principle for the sake of continued creativeness – or some such theory? It is therefore necessary to have the whole intervening series. Only through the intervention of the series can one arrive at the ultimate conceptual specification. The distance between first type and final anti-type is so vast, that it could never be seized unless the whole history of mythology intervened.

Fourth, and now we come to the final purpose of this method of interpretation, one can turn back from the anti-type and bestow a 'metaphysical' meaning on the original type. In this case one can now dispense with the intervening series and read the ultimate meaning of the original event, of which the earliest and most unspecified myth was the first slightly specified divergence, in the light of the final anti-type. In this sense, the presence of myth makes a metaphysical interpretation of the natural world possible. If one looks at the killing of an animal, one cannot attribute any meaning to it over and beyond the meaning which this particular event possesses: e.g., a man or another animal needs food. But if one looks upon it in the light of the theory that God is the world and that the world must kill itself in order to create the next phase, the killing of the animal can be understood 'metaphysically'.

The final conclusion, therefore, is that the typological as against the structural interpretation of mythology is not only non-functional in its method but also non-functional in its aim. Lévi-Strauss's view that the structuralist interpretation makes it possible for the conflict between death and life, incest and exogamy, to be 'resolved' implies squarely that ultimately mythology performs a certain function in certain societies in which these conflicts are experienced to be troublesome. By contrast, the typological method leads to nothing more (and, one might add, to nothing less) than a metaphysical interpretation of the natural world in which we live. This interpretation has no function in any particular society but helps some minds achieve greater clarity as to the meaning and purpose of existence. It does so by making use of the human mind's tendency to construct myths out of reports of natural events and to specify them more and more until they are so highly specified that they can be transformed into abstract concepts. In conclusion one might say that the phenomenon of myth itself, its inherent tendency towards progressive specification, provides a chance for the mind to understand itself. In this view, the mind's own life-story provides the material by which the mind can reveal to itself its true nature, which is to understand the world metaphysically rather than naturally. Is this what Aristotle meant when he announced, cryptically, that the mind thinks itself?

SEVEN

MYTHS AND METAPHYSICS

Once we understand that myths reveal themselves in typological series, we can also understand that they do more than that. They not only exhibit their own meaning if one follows them forward to the most specific version they take but also enable us to see the natural events from which they were first deflected in an entirely new light. For they can be re-projected on the initial event.[1]

The process is simple and almost mechanical. A highly specific version of a myth can be used as a stencil and superimposed upon the original, natural events from which the earliest and least specific version was deflected. Consider the following example. In the myth of the sacrificial death of Jesus Christ we have a story that tells us that death precedes resurrection. In its more specifically semi-theological or semi-metaphysical version, this is summed up conceptually as the doctrine that death precedes life, surrender precedes gain. Originally, in its simplest and least specific version, the story was a simple and modest deflection from a natural event, an everyday occurrence of death. The everyday occurrence, though infinitely common, is completely meaningless. It happens every day. It causes grief and suffering. But it has no significance as it happens and is contemplated by men. But now try the re-projection. If we use the more specific version of the sacrificial death and resurrection of Jesus Christ, let alone the even more specific semi-theological doctrine that death precedes life, as a stencil and superimpose it upon the natural event, the natural event can be read in a new light. It will cease to be a commonplace occurrence and receive its meaning from the stencil. It can now be seen as the *type* of the sacrificial death which precedes resurrection and it can be interpreted as an instance of the doctrine that death precedes life; surrender, gain.

The re-projection of the top of the series is a feed-back of metaphysics to nature. It is as if the abstract conceptual doctrine were a stencil. Nature is then seen through the slots of stencils provided by metaphysical doctrine. If one thinks of the re-projection as seeing nature through the slots of stencils, it is clear that one cannot derive the metaphysical doctrines from nature without the intermediate steps of myths. Hence the comparatively great abortiveness of all efforts at natural theology. But the metaphysical doctrines can illuminate nature or parts of it by allowing light to pass through the slots of the stencils. The parts of nature thus lit up will remain parts of nature; but form a pattern or shape very different from the appearance of nature in the raw. The parts thus lit up can be said to verify or provide evidence in favour of the metaphysical doctrines. But since one could never obtain those parts without the appropriate stencil, nature as it appears without the stencil cannot possibly lend support to any theological or metaphysical doctrine.

The illumination due to the slots in the stencil operates right down the series. The conceptualised doctrine at the top allows us to see the uppermost, most specified myth in a certain light and bestows a certain meaning on it. This myth, in turn, will act as a stencil to the next myth down, and so forth, until we reach the least specific, bottom myth of the series and so on to nature. This accounts for the fact that one and the same myth, e.g. the story of Noah, drunk in the vineyard, can be made to appear to have a number of different meanings. The multiplicity of its meanings is due to its position in a typological series – say, somewhere half-way. Depending on the kind of top myth or doctrine one uses as a stencil, one will get very different 'interpretations' of it. For St Augustine, the story of the drunk and naked Noah is a figure of Christ. For Simone Weil, it is an instance of Dionysian ecstasy.[2] In spite of the differences in interpretation, there is no dispute between St Augustine and Simone Weil. The phenomenon is due to the fact that the myth is fairly unspecified and receives its meaning from above, i.e. from the myths that are on top of it in the series of progressive specifications. For it is not the type that defines the meaning of the anti-type; but the anti-type which defines the meaning of the type by re-projecting it. The different interpretations of the Noah myth derive from the differences in the stencils used.

One can go further and generalise the theory that conceptualised myths are the top of a typological series and argue that *all* metaphysical concepts must be so derived. By their very nature, the metaphysical doctrines that time is unreal; that the World is One; that spatial extension is an illusion; that love is the motive power of the Universe; that consciousness or mind are diffused throughout the realm of matter; that consciousness is material; and many others, cannot be derived, and never have claimed to be derived, from the direct and immediate observation of nature. It is therefore imaginable that all these metaphysical concepts are conceptualisations of mythical series. One could thus make an entirely new approach to the meaning and significance of metaphysical theories by trying to derive them from mythologies.

We owe the finest and most sensitive presentation of this relationship between myth and metaphysics to Heinrich Zimmer's *Myths and Symbols in Indian Art and Civilization*. Zimmer confined himself to India. On a larger and more ambitious scale, we have a project initiated by Alan W. Watts under the title *Patterns of Myth* designed to explore and present systematically the connections between mythical imagery and metaphysical doctrines.[3]

Many years ago Rudolf Carnap[4] wrote that 'metaphysical propositions – like lyrical verses – have only an expressive function, but no representative function', thus adding much weight to the contempt for metaphysics which is so widespread in the modern world. The social and economic pressures which generate this contempt are unpleasant but intelligible. But Carnap's argument is unforgivable because it is superficial. The truth of the matter is that metaphysical propositions, like all other propositions, have a representative function. They represent myths. They are about myths and are the conceptual summaries of myths. Their truth can be tested like the truth of all other propositions by reference to the myths they are about. Myths, as will be shown later, have an expressive function. But it does not follow that myths and metaphysical propositions are to be equated. The relation between metaphysics and emotions is therefore oblique. Emotions are expressed in myths and myths are propositionally represented by metaphysics. All together form a typological series. Many philosophers, both before and after Carnap, unaware of the typological series and the changing qualities between its several terms as the series proceeds from unspecified images through specified images to high levels of conceptual abstraction, have simply lumped metaphysics and myth together and believed that both are non-representational and express emotions. Accurate observation, however, shows that, while there is a relationship between emotion and metaphysics, it is oblique. As the elaboration of the series proceeds, expression changes into representation. Metaphysical propositions are not representative of emotions but of myths. The relationship between metaphysics and emotion is oblique because of the intervention of myth. To make the point clearer, I would add two random examples. Plato was quite conscious of the fact that most of his metaphysical doctrines were not derived by logical reasoning but were conceptual formulations of the vision of the world contained in the myths scattered throughout his writings. He is quite unconcerned about the provenance of these myths. But he is very concerned about the specific relationship which exists between his metaphysical doctrines and these myths. The doctrines are in fact abstract statements of these myths and the myths provide the justification and validity for these doctrines. Without the relevant myths, his scepticism in regard to our knowledge of particulars and his doctrine that we recognise the universal because we remember what we have seen before our entombment in our body appear hardly plausible. Subsequent philosophers have tried to examine the truth of these doctrines without reference to the myths provided and on the basis of which he established them. As one might expect, they have only been moderately successful and in many cases have reached the conclusion that they cannot really go along with Plato. This is not surprising, for they have chosen to leave out the evidence which Plato adduced to justify his conclusions.[5] Or consider a completely different case. Jean-Paul Sartre propagated a whole philosophical movement with the contention that man is fated to be free and that man's existence precedes his essence. Examined in cold blood and in the light of pure reason, this contention must remain at best a half-truth. But it so happens that Sartre himself has provided a picture of the world which occupies in his thought a place analogous to the place occupied by myth in Plato's thought. In his novels, especially in *Roads to Freedom*, he has provided the evidence which makes his doctrine of freedom highly convincing. His novels provide much more persuasive evidence for his metaphysics than his own reasoned attempt in *Being and Nothingness*.[6] One can say for both Plato and Sartre that their metaphysical doctrines may not be universally valid but that they are true, abstract formulations of the evidence contained in Plato's myths and in Sartre's novels.

The re-projection of the highly specific version of myth upon nature reveals, therefore, features and shapes in nature which nature herself does not automatically exhibit and which are not visible to the naked eye. Nevertheless, once this ability of myth to act as a stencil is granted, it is not difficult to see that the meaning made manifest through re-projection was implicit in nature all along. It took the long detour through the formation of myth into a typological series to make it apparent. If we describe the ultimate specific and conceptualised myth as metaphysical truth, and nature, from which the initial, non-specific myth was first deflected, as the raw material, we can conclude that the typological series in which myth presents itself historically, mediates between nature and truth. There is no obvious and explicit relationship between nature and truth in this sense. No amount of twisting and turning of one's contemplation of the natural event of death would reveal anything other than the positive and laconic conclusion that life precedes death and that 'all life death does end and each day dies with sleep' (Gerard Manley Hopkins). All that can be learnt from nature is natural truth, that is, the positive statement that life precedes death. But if one allows myth to mediate, that is, if one considers myth in its typological appearance and then re-projects it upon nature, nature will yield a different picture. It will suddenly bear out the truth of the mythical version that death precedes life and that the truth is not what nature by itself and independently exhibited, but that the truth is the other way round. The development of mythical imagery by transposition, re-shuffling and progressive typological specification casts a veil over nature – not to hide it, but, a seeming paradox, to enable us to see all the more clearly the existing possible patterns and contours which are not apparent to the naked eye and which can only be seen with the help of that veil. This is why Goethe said that the poet receives 'der Dichtung Schleier aus der Hand der Wahrheit' – the veil of poetry is bestowed by the hand of truth.

EIGHT

METAPHYSICS AND SYMBOLS

If myths display their own meaning, they must be taken to exist in
their own right, even as trees and mountains exist. They are part
of the furniture of the universe rather than messages or means to
certain ends. In this case, it is necessary to inquire more carefully
into their ontological status. Myths are no more than extreme cases
of metaphor. This simple truth is all too often completely ignored or
overlooked; or, when it is noticed, no special importance is attributed
to it. Almost every writer on the subject devotes much space to a
discussion of the distinctions between myth and legend, folk-tale
and dream. The attempts to distinguish between these various genres
of stories are interesting and perhaps even useful in some contexts.
But formally, all these stories are instances of metaphor.

'Metaphor,' wrote Herbert Read, 'is the synthesis of several complex
units into one commanding image; it is the expression of a complex
idea . . . by the sudden perception of an objective relation'.[1] Read tries
to draw our attention to the fact that in the construction of a metaphor we are putting together several originally disparate elements
into one single complex, which, by itself, cannot be found originally
in nature. The creation of metaphor presupposes a metamorphosis,
a transposition of elements into a new assembly. Although it is
often expressed in words, it consists, in the first instance, in a
transfer of separate images into a new image. It is therefore not a
purely semantic phenomenon. The question whether the transformation which lies at the basis of metaphor, the transposition of images
and eventually of words, is a discovery or an invention has frequently been debated. It seems, however, of purely academic interest.
Metaphor is an instantaneous contact of two separate images. The
bringing together may be an invention; but the stumbling upon
their initial existence is a discovery and the appropriateness of bring-

ing this discovery together is, given certain compelling circumstances, a complete mixture of invention and discovery.

There is a tendency among some recent American commentators to drop the distinction between metaphor and simile.[2] Against this, I would argue that the distinction between simile and metaphor is fundamental. A simile is a mere rhetorical device. It likens something to something else. By establishing similarities, it does not create a new image but, on the contrary, keeps the separate elements, no matter how much they are alike, firmly apart. If my love is *like* a red rose, then my love and the red rose are similar but separate. If, however, in genuine metaphor, my love is a red rose, the two images become fused and a new, third, image is created by a process which is a mixture of invention and discovery.

A story is a set of relations; or, more precisely, it places a series of events in certain relationships. The significant feature of the stories we are concerned with, whether they be folk-tales or myths proper, legends or dreams, is that the events they consist of always appear in non-normal relations. People are larger than life-size, dwarves fly through the air, heroes are immortal, the dead return to life. In short, the normal position in which events stand to one another is changed. Events, it seems, are re-shuffled like a pack of cards and thus they emerge in relationships in which they do not normally stand to one another. This kind of re-shuffling, however, is precisely the kind of transformation that takes place when a metaphor is created. When we speak of the Lion of Judah, we take the image of a lion in the forest and of a ruler in a council chamber and re-shuffle them. We get rid of the forest and we get rid of the council chamber and thus by re-connecting the remaining features, we get the Lion of Judah. In this sense, it makes little difference whether a story is a legend or a myth, a folk-tale or a dream. In a formal analysis, they all must be classed as sustained metaphors.

Metaphors are much more ubiquitous than is commonly supposed. To my knowledge there exists no statistical survey of the question; but one need not hesitate to assert that a very large percentage of the statements of which our daily speech consists are metaphors rather than literal statements. That is to say, they are not statements in which events are recounted as they 'normally' appear, but statements in which events are re-shuffled. The ubiquity of metaphor in daily speech is proved when one's glance ranges from such simple expressions as 'to switch the light out' to more sophisticated exclamations as 'you are not in your right mind' or to descriptions of such common tasks as 'washing up'. It would take very little argument to prove that if we eschewed all metaphorical expressions and not only the more self-consciously poetical ones created by parti- cularly perceptive and sensitive people, daily language would cease to exist and human communication would become impossible. It follows then that the daily universe described or referred to in our common speech is not at all 'normal' and that we live day in and day out in a world described by metaphor rather than by literal statements.[3] It is therefore no exaggeration to say that the world in which we live is much more mythical than we suppose; or that the world of myth is not nearly as weird as most of us like to imagine. All this follows from the formal similarity between myth and metaphor.

The question which arises next is why the metaphor that a giant destroyed a castle is not a 'normal' story. The destruction of castles by men is a normal story. But the story that the castle was destroyed by a giant is not. The image of the giant is clearly due to re-shuffling. One takes a large tree and abstracts the size; one takes a man, and abstracts his human height; and finally one combines the size of the tree with the figure of the man and gets a giant. For such a re- shuffling operation to be performed, one needs the intervention of the human mind. As things normally appear in nature, the height of a human being cannot be pushed aside and the figure combined with the height of a tree. On the contrary, normally speaking, one can establish a nature-given relationship between the height of a human being and the height of any given tree by saying that the tree is, for example, four times as high as the human being. Such a state- ment is a literal statement and expresses the relationships in which things stand to one another in the world of nature. Ideally, no human mind need interfere between the human being and the tree. The relationship between their heights is given by nature and can be said to be autochthonous. In nature all objects and events are related to each other naturally. They appear in certain relation- ships which are unalterable whether a human mind is watching or not. This is not to say that a human mind cannot multiply or diversify these relationships. There is a natural relationship between the human retina and a tree. But we can interpose a ground lens

and thus alter the relationship between retina and tree. The altera-
tion, however, is still a natural one and should not be confused with
re-shuffling. Again, we can interpose a camera, take an X-ray photograph of the tree, develop the film and project it on a screen and
get an oscillator to record the light fluctuations on the screen and
have those fluctuations in turn translated into numerical values
by a computer and inscribed on a punch-card. And the marks on the
punch-card can be seen by the retina. Thanks to the ingenuity of
the human mind, the tree is transformed into a series of holes. The
process can be reversed, but its steps cannot be altered, for the
relationships in which they stand to one another are fixed, natural
relationships. Although there seem to be no limits to the ingenuity
with which the human mind can interpose parts of nature between,
say, the retina and the tree, it cannot alter the relationships which
exist naturally between the various parts, even though nature
herself has not immediately or obviously placed all her parts into
positions or places in which they exhibit a relationship. Whatever the
role of the ingenuity of the human mind, the role is limited to
exhibiting natural relationships and to creating new natural relationships. The human mind, no matter how ingenious, can, in other
words, not interfere with the autochthonous relationships that exist
in nature.

As soon as the human mind, instead of being ingenious, ceases to
be disinterested and becomes aware of its qualitative emotions and
feelings, it begins to gaze upon the, say, human figure and the tree
in a new light. I would like to suggest that we call this interested –
as opposed to disinterested – way of looking at the world, the way of
looking *sub specie essentiae*. The expression *essentia* here is not to
remind us of essence; but of being. That is, of the state of being a
person feels himself to be in. So that when we look on the world
while we are conscious of the emotions and feelings we have while
we are looking, we are looking at the world through the matrix of
these emotions or feelings. We are looking while we are conscious
of the particular state of being we are in. We are looking while we
are conscious of how we feel ourselves to be. Hence the expression
'looking *sub specie essentiae*'. When we are looking *sub specie essentiae*, there arises the possibility of a re-shuffling – an urge towards
metaphor rather than towards literal statement expressing the autochthonous relation in which the tree and the human being stand to-

wards one another. This was first clearly perceived by Rousseau in his essays on the origin of language[4] and has since been accepted by countless modern writers, including Lévi-Strauss.

The creation of metaphor seems to be dictated by a special condition of the human mind. It has long been observed that there is a vast difference between shedding tears and the feeling of sadness, between blushing and a sense of shame. But the implications of this difference have not always been clearly understood. They have a special bearing upon the necessity for metaphor.

When a person sheds tears, someone else may legitimately conclude that that person feels sad. But this conclusion is very different from the sadness experienced by the person who sheds tears. The person who sheds tears can, of course, confirm the conclusion reached by the other man and confess that he is indeed sad. But, and this is the crucial point, the tear-shedder's own admission of his own sadness is just as different from the feeling of sadness as the observing person's legitimate if tentative inference that the tear-shedder is sad. This means that if the tear-shedder says that he is sad, he is making a literal statement about his own condition. But it so happens that this literal statement is in no way different from the statement of the outside observer that the tear-shedder is sad. Like the outside observer's statement, it does not reflect the feeling of sadness. It merely confirms what the outside observer was able to infer from the tears. In fact, however, the tear-shedder is experiencing sadness. He is undergoing an experience which is completely different from the experience of the outside observer whose experience can be described as tear-watching. But if the tear-shedder says no more than 'I am sad' he is, linguistically, saying something that is identical with the statement of the observer. But in actual fact, to do justice to his own emotion, he ought to be saying something completely different. If he confines himself to a literal description to the effect that he is sad, he is behaving as if he himself were also no more than an outside observer of his own sadness. But we know that he is not. Hence the insufficiency, for the tear-shedder, of literal description.

It is worth mentioning, although it is now only a matter of purely historical interest, that earlier this century a very strenuous effort was made by many philosophers to grant a complete monopoly of meaningfulness to literal statements. These statements were called 'protocol-statements' and it was suggested that any statement which could not be translated into a protocol-statement was a meaningless statement. These efforts have almost completely been abandoned and a large number of considerations have been urged against the claim that literal statements should enjoy a monopoly. The preceding argument is no more than yet another reason for the destruction of that monopoly.

It is worth adding that the argument also derives its inspiration in an indirect sense from a line of thought nowadays forcefully represented by Piaget. It sees the self-regulating organism, in following its own internal laws, as going beyond mere adaptation. The organism, including its genetic system, transcends any restriction to static units of heredity. This formative surplus becomes the creative imagination and makes man pass beyond the mechanical interplay between his genetic system and his environment.[5]

If feelings are not adequately expressed by statements which are formally, like statements made by outside observers of, say, tears, it follows that feelings can be adequately expressed or referred to only by symbols. That is to say, feelings must be symbolised rather than described literally. A person who feels sad, instead of stating blandly that he feels sad, ought to point to an event or an object and designate it as a symbol of his feeling. The symbol in this sense is what T. S. Eliot described as the 'objective correlative'.[6] It goes without saying that the objective correlative thus designated is not a cause of the feeling-state. It is more correct to say that the objective correlative is the symbol of the feeling-state. The nature of this symbolic relationship, however, is not easy to describe. One could say that the symbol expresses the feeling-state. If one points at a weeping willow tree and exclaims, 'There! this is how I feel!', one is expressing one's state of feeling without describing it literally. The weeping willow tree is the objective correlative, the image which gives definition and meaning to the feeling-state. It is not its cause; but it can be said to express it. But the word 'express' in this sense is clearly itself metaphorical. Literally, we express juice from an orange or liquid from a container. The use of the word 'express' in any other sense – even the substitution of 'expression' for 'word' – is metaphorical. When the weeping willow tree is designated as the objective correlative of a feeling-state, it makes perfectly good sense to speak of expression. But such speech is not literal.

It lies in the nature of the case that one should experience difficulty in finding the right nomenclature. A feeling-state, to begin with, cannot be described *qua* feeling-state. It is part of or possibly the whole of our own personal inwardness. As such it is impossible to focus on it, to concentrate on it, because it has no definition. And yet, just as its presence is indubitable, its content cannot be referred to. In order to designate its content – in order to say that it is a state of sadness or of indefinite distance from other people or from our own selves, we have to point to an objective image. It is here that T. S. Eliot's terminology seems so helpful. The feeling-state is a state of purblind consciousness, tenuous and unnameable as we experience it, but definable and a consciousness of something as soon as we relate it to an objective correlative. And yet we have to guard against some of the implications of T. S. Eliot's terminology, all the more so as he himself took pains not to guard against them. According to T. S. Eliot, the emotion cannot receive definition and cannot be referred to and cannot arise as a definite emotion of this or that unless there is an objective correlative. So far, so good. But he goes on to state that whenever the objective correlative is stated, the corresponding emotion will be aroused. With this statement he goes beyond the problem of definition and says that there is a causal relationship between the objective correlative and the emotion it defines. This view not only implies a certain mechanicalness in the relation between the emotion and the objective correlative but also indicates causality. And last, not least, it suggests that the emotion can be named by itself so that it is possible to assess whether a certain objective correlative is adequate or not. All these implications and suggestions must be rejected. The feeling-state cannot be named as it occurs. It lies in its very nature to be undefined and inchoate. It receives a name and meaning from its symbol. There is good sense in calling that symbol its objective correlative, provided one does not link the notion to the mechanistic and causal implications attributed to it by T. S. Eliot. The feeling-state is something very much like the *Bewusstseinslage* discussed and investigated by the German school of Würzburg psychologists and so valiantly and persuasively defended by Findlay in his Gifford Lectures.[7]

The term 'symbol' is used here in two slightly different but complementary senses. In the first instance, it is used in a sense that is close to the sense in which it is used in symbolic logic. In this sense, a symbol is an object or event or image which stands for a state of feeling or mind. One can say that in this sense the symbol is a substitute for the state symbolised – except for one circumstance which makes the notion of simple substitution very complicated. This circumstance concerns what we will call the poverty effect. One single symbol, we will observe, can stand for quite a variety of emotions or states of mind and therefore symbolises any one of them both imperfectly and equivocally. A tree in blossom, for example, can symbolise both joy and peace, or a feeling of spring and awakening and growth – all of which are very different from one another. The symbol, in this sense, is too poor to do justice to the many nuances of feeling that can be experienced or to the many qualities our emotions assume. (It is worth noticing at this point that the expressions 'peace' and 'awakening' do not refer literally to the states of mind symbolised; but are yet further symbols, i.e. events. Nevertheless, they have to be employed here in this elliptical manner for otherwise it would be impossible to indicate that there are differences between one emotion and another and that any one symbol can refer to a whole range of emotions.) In the second instance, 'symbol' is used to describe an object or event or an image of an object or event that is artificially constructed or put together. In this second sense there is no simple substitution; or better, the symbol that is substituted for the state of mind is an artificially contrived entity, something like a metaphor. An artificially put together symbol like a fish playing a violin or an outsize man hurling thunderbolts, is essentially a metaphor rather than an object one stumbles across in one's daily, mundane life. It is a substitute for a feeling; but an elaborated and artificially made substitute. Unlike the non-elaborated one, it is not subject to the poverty effect. On the contrary. A metaphor stands for a feeling in a very precise way and the more elaborate the metaphor, the more precise the symbolisation. If the symbol in the first sense is subject to the poverty effect, the symbol in the second sense is subject to an abundance effect. One feeling-state can be symbolised adequately, unequivocally and precisely by a large number of very different contrived symbols (metaphors); for it is possible to contrive or construct a large number of equivalent but different metaphors. When we use 'symbol' in the first sense, we get a surfeit of emotion symbolised by one and the same symbol. When we use 'symbol' in the second sense, we get a surfeit of symbols (metaphors) to symbolise any one state of feeling. But the two senses of 'symbol' are complementary because a symbol in the first sense can be the type of a symbol in the second sense. Of this more later. The poverty effect renders the simple object fairly inefficient as a symbol. The abundance effect, however, creates a new order of problems, but at least does not render the symbol vague and imprecise. Hence we conclude that the metaphor which is essentially a transposition or transfer, an assembly of naturally separate and/or disparate elements, is the symbol *par excellence*, while the simple non-metaphorical symbol is nothing but a first rough stab at symbolisation. Only the metaphor functions efficiently as a symbol.

But before proceeding to an examination of metaphors as symbols *par excellence*, another remark about symbolisation as such is needed. We have said that a feeling-state can be expressed adequately only by a symbol. A symbol does not have to be a metaphor. Any image will do. We have also argued that the relationship between an image which acts as a symbol and the state of mind which is symbolised is *not* a causal relationship, but one of ascription. The symbolising image is an objective correlative. In order to bring out the full implications of this view, a further reflection is necessary. When I think of a tree or dream of a tree or wish for a tree, we are all agreed that the tree in question is an image. But when I actually see a real tree in front of my eyes, many people would be inclined to call this tree a genuinely 'perceived' tree and would be reluctant to refer to it as an 'image'. I would like to argue that it will be helpful to neglect the difference between the tree as an image and the tree as a perception. My reasons for the argument are as follows. While there can be no doubt as to the important physiological difference between the image and the perception, one can also look upon the matter in a different way. One can obliterate the distinction between perception and image by thinking of the perception as an image in which one sees oneself perceiving the tree. If one thinks of one's perception of the tree, there is no difficulty in designating this thought as an image. It may be a second-order image; or one might like to describe it, in order to distinguish it from the first-order images, as a subjective image. The first-order image, in which the tree appears as a hope or a dream or a thought, is an objective image. It is an image *tout court*. The second-order image is a subjective image because the subject who is perceiving the tree has to figure in it as part of the image. Whatever the implications of the distinction for epistemology and the theory of perception, it will be helpful for our present purposes to neglect the distinction or, at least, to attribute no further importance to it. An image, whether it is subjective or objective in the sense here described is, nevertheless, an image. And as an image it can be used as a symbol or an objective correlative.

The role and importance of images, whether subjective or objective, for an understanding of human feelings cannot be questioned. Before proceeding with the argument, however, we should consider briefly a very strange side-effect of the insight that images are a vital element in our understanding of our own emotions. The role which images play is the role of objective correlatives. Their *raison d'être* is their power to symbolise states of feeling. But as so often, people in this case have been tempted to regard images as ends in themselves. They have frequently – one might even say more frequently than not – given way to the temptation to elaborate images according to internal criteria. They have detached them from their symbolic function and explored and extended them according to these criteria. The elaboration of a *typos* image into anti-types gives rise to a typological series. But the direction of the series is controlled by the need to give more clarity and precision and greater definition to the feeling-state symbolised by the original *typos*. Unless this external criterion is kept in mind, the elaboration of the typological series loses its point. This is all too frequently overlooked.

There are two very obviously available internal criteria for the elaboration of typological series. One is aesthetics; and the other, logic. The employment of the first, to the exclusion of every other consideration, has given rise to art; and the employment of the other, to the exclusion of all other considerations, to the emergence of theology. One can take any set of images and elaborate and refine them according to purely formal aesthetic criteria. Every image is a visual phenomenon and as such it can be painted or sculpted. One can then proceed and develop the painting into a definite style by using no considerations other than purely aesthetic ones. The result is a school of art. Its products will edify and can even inspire. In the end, the school must tend towards some form of formal abstraction. At that point, its values become purely aesthetic and can be judged only in purely aesthetic terms. Whatever its merits, it has become divorced from the principal purpose of imagery and usually ceases to throw light on states of feeling. The products of the school cease to operate as objective correlatives.[8]

The same argument applies to the verbal description of images. Any image can more or less successfully be described in words. Once it is so described, it is possible to go to work on the sentences with the help of logic and explore the logical implications of these sentences. In this way one will obtain, instead of a typological series of stories that act as objective correlatives to emotions or states of feeling, a series of statements which follow logically from the verbal description of one or of several images. This kind of logical exploration of verbally described images not only leads to a set of theological propositions which are, in themselves, quite meaningless even though they are logically derived from verbal descriptions of images; but also to a number of theological puzzles. Thus theologians have for centuries wondered how God can be omniscient when men are supposed to be endowed with free will; or how God can be both good and all-powerful when the world is so full of evil. Logic insists that He is either not good or not all-powerful if evil is allowed to go unpunished. Consider the following example. At a certain stage in the development of Biblical mythic imagery, God was described as immutable. At another stage there appeared the image of God becoming man, i.e. of the Incarnation. In view of what we have said about the typological progression of imagery, this is perfectly understandable. The original *typos* is the image of somebody creating something. Then comes a specification: the creator is made divine and invested with a number of majestic attributes of which immutability is one; and the thing created is made into the totality of the world. Next follows a further specification. The Creator is also all-loving and compassionate and thus comes the image of the Incarnation. But to those theologians who do not appreciate the typological progression of mythic imagery and who apply logical criteria in order to develop further images, there now arises a problem. If God is immutable, they say, he cannot possibly 'become' a man, for the image of the Incarnation (God becomes man) cannot be deduced from the image of immutability. There is no need to go over the attempts that have been made to cope with this alleged problem. The problem arises only on the assumption that the progression of mythic images takes place according to logical criteria – that is, an image must be deducible from its predecessors, or, more correctly, a verbal description of an image should imply the verbal description of its successor. The problem disappears when one understands that images, including mythic images, are related typologically and that each successive image emerges as a further specification of its predecessor and that the rationale of the specification consists in the drive towards more precise definition of a state of consciousness. The objective correlatives of these states (or their verbal descriptions) do not form a chain of logically deducible mythic images (or, more precisely, of propositions verbally describing mythic images), but a chain of typologically related images. It must be clear then that the application of logic to the elaboration of the typological series amounts to the application of a purely internal criterion. If images are described in words, logic can be applied; for logic is applicable to all language. But the catch is that the *raison d'être* of images lies outside images and that the elaboration of the typological series ought to be controlled by the external factor, the presence of emotions or states of feeling. The images must continue, no matter how typologically elaborate they become, to be controlled by their power to symbolise these feeling-states. If the elaboration takes place in terms of a purely internal criterion such as logic, it ceases to be meaningful. The ultimate formulations of theology, like the ultimate abstractions of art, no matter how logical and how aesthetically beautiful, have ceased to be controlled by states of feeling and have therefore lost their purpose as objective correlatives.

There is no question that at the present time more and more thoughtful people have resisted the temptation to use the purely internal criterion of logic for elaborating verbally formulated images into typological series. For reasons which we cannot here consider, the employment of the internal criterion of logic to the typological series has failed to hold our attention. This is a desirable development and the immediate result of this development is that we have come to prefer poetry to formal theology. For poetry refuses to use the internal criterion of logic in its elaboration and concatenation of images. Theologians take hold of an image (e.g. the creation of the world), describe it in words that form sentences, and then deduce other sentences with the help of the rules of logic. Poets, by contrast, seize an image and either specify it or juxtapose it to another image in accordance with the requirements of feeling-states. The one series of images hangs together because of the logical relationship between the sentences that describe them; and the other series hangs together because each image is a symbol for a state of mind, so that the rationale for the series of images is not provided by the logical relationship of the sentences that describe them or the inherent beauty of their visual appearance, but by the fact that the images are a typological series which progressively defines and specifies a state of feeling. While formal theology has lost its fascination, abstract art has not. There is no reason why people should not produce abstract art. For that matter, there is no reason why people should not indulge in the pastime of formal theology. The only point worth making is that the pursuit of these forms of art and theology is a superfluous extension of the use we can make of imagery. The great pity of it is that many people, conscious of the possible but pointless extension of imagery according to its own inherent criteria, have tended to conclude that imagery as a whole is pointless. They have therefore tended to attribute greater value to literal pursuits, and have thus poured out the baby with the bath-water. In this way they debar themselves from ever reaching a fuller and clearer awareness of their emotions and states of feeling. The arrangement of imagery into typological series is necessary for the improvement of the degree of precision with which the objective correlatives help us to be aware of emotions. The only requirement is that typological elaboration should follow the rationale of states of feeling and should not be controlled by criteria internal either to the verbal description (logic) or to the visual appearance (beauty) of images. It is only imagery extended according to its own inherent criteria and elaborated according to internal considerations of logic and beauty, and thus divorced from its essential function of symbolising states of feeling, which is superfluous. But imagery and the typological development of imagery is not.

The natural world in which we live and which surrounds us is full of potential symbols. Anything that happens in it, any object it contains, can serve as a symbol for a feeling. But the natural world's objects and events are limited in number and therefore, if one takes one's symbols straight as one finds them ready made, they do not suffice to symbolise the almost infinite variety of feelings, their nuances and shades and their subtle differentiations. The natural world, in brief, is too poor to act as an adequate store of symbols. This poverty is nowhere better and more poignantly described than

F

by Henry James's short story *The Real Thing*. In this story a painter, commissioned to illustrate a book, needs a man and a woman to pose as a bourgeois couple. In answer to his advertisement, he engages a genuine bourgeois couple who are in financial difficulties and hope to earn money by modelling. At first sight, the painter could wish for nothing better than the real thing. But he soon discovers that with the genuineness of his models his inspiration departs. Eventually he makes his valet dress up in bourgeois clothes and finds that his inspiration returns.

The objects and events available in the natural world are limited in number; but feelings, although they can be classed roughly into a finite number of categories, are, on closer inspection, infinitely variable. Hence, the natural world does not suffice and has to be supplemented. I would like to suggest that this phenomenon be called the poverty effect of the natural world. It comes about in the following way. Any natural event which is designated as a symbol or objective correlative is an imprecise symbol in that it can refer to more than one feeling-state. A weeping willow can mean the sadness due to a bereavement as well as a sadness owing to romantic languor. The two feeling-states in question, sadness of bereavement and sadness of romantic languor, are experientially and intro-spectively poles apart. The weeping willow is a viable symbol pre-sented to us by nature and might do as an objective correlative at a rough stab. But on closer inspection it will not do because it is equivocal in that it can refer to a wide range of actually very different feeling-states. For this reason it is clear that, for purposes of symbol-isation, natural events are subject to the poverty effect. The world of nature is too poor to offer the full range of objective correlatives required by the vast richness of all human emotional nuances.

There is a very simple and, in fact, only one simple method for supplementing the existing store of symbols. To supplement, we must re-shuffle the objects and events presented to us by the natural world in our natural experience. By re-shuffling, it is possible to multiply the objects and events of the natural world without limit. By taking a piece or a feature here and a piece there and by detach-ing them from their natural context and re-assembling them together, there is no limit to the new series of images and stories one can create. This re-shuffling, as we have seen above, is basically similar to the re-shuffling involved in the creation of metaphor. The re-shuffling, however, is not arbitrary. It is a putting together of separate elements so that they can act as a symbol more adequate to a feeling-state than any one of the elements as it stands in its natural context. The awareness of feeling-state, therefore, is the guarantee against arbitrary re-shuffling. It imposes a strict control on the emergence of metaphor and guards against riotous fantasy. For this reason, metaphors which are purely fanciful or whimsical or idiosyncratic do not survive. The longevity of myth and its spell-binding quality across millennia is an assurance that it adequately symbolises genuine feeling-states. In this respect false myths are like treason: they never prosper.

We can now elaborate a little on the casual justification of metaphysical doctrines intimated above. Most metaphysical doctrines, far from transgressing the bounds of intelligibility, as so many philosophers from Kant to Wittgenstein have been wont to assert, are conceptual conversions of long chains of progressively elaborated and typologically related metaphors – the first link of which is no more than an image of a simple factual truth performing the function of the type. The departure from plain factual and ordinarily natural truth which is contained in metaphysical doctrines and which makes them notoriously difficult if not impossible to test is therefore not an arbitrary transgression of the bounds of intelligibility but a very methodical deflection of natural experience in the service of intelligibility. The deflection is systematically controlled by the need to create increasingly precise objective correlatives to our states of feeling. It loses its justification if there is no reference to them, and provides a higher degree of intelligibility than is afforded by our observation of the natural world by providing the objective correlatives without which the states of feeling, incapable of literal description, would remain mute, opaque, undefined and inchoate. This theory of the nature and status of metaphysical doctrines is also able to explain why metaphysical doctrines are not empirically testable. It is notorious that the fact that they are not so testable has led to the widely held belief that they are senseless and superfluous. On the present theory, however, it is perfectly clear that they are not empirically testable not because they are meaningless; but because they are derived from ordinary experience (propositions about which *are* empirically testable) *via* long chains or typologically elaborated myths and/or metaphors. Alternately, one can use Kantian terminology and say that metaphysical doctrines are synthetic *a posteriori* – that is, posterior to mythical imagery; and that they are related to nature *via* the imagery. Kant's identification of metaphysics with synthetic *a priori* propositions is, therefore, to be rejected. One can share his scepticism in regard to synthetic *a priori* propositions without sharing his scepticism in regard to metaphysics. For metaphysical knowledge, like all other knowledge, is *a posteriori*. All one need do is to bear in mind what it is posterior to.

There exists, therefore, a hiatus between ordinary experience and metaphysical doctrine – but this hiatus is filled in by myths and metaphors and once one follows their typological progression, the hiatus disappears. The disappearance, however, does not make the metaphysical doctrine directly empirically testable. It merely shows the manner in which it is linked to ordinary experience and thus dispels the idea that it is meaningless. A feeling of pristine innocence can be symbolised by a myth about a virgin immaculately conceived; by a myth of a virgin emerging from the foam of waves; or by a myth of shepherds worshipping a child in a crib. The abundance effect is responsible for the fact that one and the same feeling-state can be given a wide variety of objective correlatives. These objective correlatives or symbols are equivalent. This equivalence does not mean that they are substantially similar in content; but that they all refer to the same feeling-state even though they are in content and substance very different. The failure to appreciate the abundance effect has led to many unnecessary confusions in the interpretation of mythology and has created a large number of pseudo-problems. All too often interpreters confine their attention to the content of a myth and fail to see that there may be a significant equivalence, in some respects, between a myth about a virgin born from the foam of the waves and a myth about a newly born child worshipped by shepherds. The equivalence is not direct but depends on the feeling-state of which the two myths are alternative objective correlatives. The confusion and the pseudo-problems arise all the more readily because it is, by the nature of the case, not possible to determine literally that two very different myths may be two different objective correlatives of one and the same feeling-state. This comes about because the feeling-state cannot be described literally except in a very rough and ready fashion – in the present example one can merely say that it is a feeling-state of primeval innocence. But as we have seen above, literal descriptions fail to do justice to the feeling-states as they are actually experienced. Hence the difficulty of pin-pointing the equivalence of the objective correlatives by stating unequivocally and precisely the nature or character of the feeling-state to which they both refer and in terms of which they are indeed equivalent.

The abundance effect, though its importance for the understanding of mythology has never been appreciated, is no new discovery. It has been known, though not named, in psychiatry for a long time. It has been observed, a long time ago, that one and the same mental, in this case, pathological, condition can find expression in a large variety of actions and fantasies, each of which is equally appropriate for the patient – so that it is almost a matter of accident which of the many possible expressions will predominate. It was observed that the mental state of *algolagnia*, in which there is a pleasurable sexual excitation surrounding terror (this is a literal description of a feeling-state – clumsy at best; and at worst, incapable of coming near the core of the genuine quality of the consciousness involved), can find expression in or can be symbolised by the death of animals or human beings, accidental or contrived, imaginary or real. Similarly, it can be expressed by the threat of destruction of property or health or the threat of death or consist in the annihilation of inanimate objects. Moreover the person who wants to express his feeling may perform the act himself or induce someone else to perform it or be simply a spectator. Or else, he may himself imagine himself to be the victim of an attack or place himself in a position where he is the victim of an attack, and so forth.[9] There is a large variety of completely different events which act as symbols for one and the same feeling-state and, most important, many of these events are quite incompatible with one another, as, for instance the subject's murder of another man and another man's murder of the subject. In spite of this incompatibility, both events are capable of symbolising the same feeling-state.

NINE

SYMBOLS AND SIGNS

A great deal of misunderstanding has resulted from the failure to see metaphor and myth as supplements, designed to add a store of symbols to the symbols provided by the natural world we experience. If myth and metaphor are *not* taken as supplements, it is easy, all too easy, to look upon them as symbols of natural events. This is precisely what has happened in many cases. A symbol like a solar deity is seen as a symbol of the sun; a symbol like a sacrifice is seen as a symbol of a communal repast. In other words, the myth or metaphor is taken to *stand for* or to *signify* the natural event.

During the nineteenth century, at the height of liberal rationalism, the practice of looking upon myths and metaphors as substitutions for genuine events enjoyed a great vogue. There would today be no need to criticise this simple substitution theory were it not for the fact that it has been revived in the writings of many sociologists and anthropologists. Robert Graves, for example, has argued that an ancient icon of the murder of Belus, in which a man plunges a dagger into a sleeping man while a smallish woman is watching in the background, is a picture of a real event. He believes that the myth that God created woman by taking a rib from Adam was substituted for the story depicted in this icon. Quite recently J. M. Allegro has caused something approaching a scandal by arguing that the Christian cross is a substitution for the cosmic mushroom from which there used to fall intoxicatingly fertile seeds and that that mushroom, in turn, was a substitution for the phallus sprouting forth or ejaculating spermatozoa. There may be truth in the observation that there is an isomorphism between the mushroom and the cross and their respective life-giving activities. But since the cross and the blessings it bestows are more specific than the mushroom and its fertilising operations, it is absurd to argue that the more specific symbol is a substitution for the less specific one in the sense that the former stands for the latter and is a sign for the latter and therefore redundant. It is equally wrong to conclude that the cross means the mushroom as if it were a sign of the mushroom. The truth of the matter is that the mushroom is a figure or type and the cross is the anti-type. In order to understand the meaning of the series one cannot just consider the anti-type the sign of the type, but one has to discover further anti-types in the series and gauge, by observing them, the direction in which the series tends. Having done this, one can take a late and highly specific anti-type and watch its feed-back to earlier less specific types and thus see what light is shed on them. In this way one will reach a conclusion diametrically opposed to Allegro. One will see that the Cross sheds light on or means the mushroom; not the other way round. Guy E. Swanson[1] has argued that spiritual beings are substitutes for certain constitutional structures of social life and has made an elaborate effort to account for the different natures of these spiritual beings in terms of the different constitutional structures of different societies. While there is something disarming in the charming simplicity of these substitution theories and in their authors' zealous claim to have discovered the event or experience or belief replaced and disguised by certain myths, we should also take a closer look at a more systematic revelation of the events concealed by mythology and metaphysics. If Topitsch lacks the flair and poetic *élan* of Graves and Allegro, his exposition has the advantage of thoroughness and wide coverage. In his *Vom Ursprung und Ende der Metaphysik*,[2] Topitsch presented a detailed account of the origin of metaphysical thought in which he demonstrated that metaphysical doctrines, which he sensibly did not distinguish too sharply from myths, were 'modelled' on ordinary experiences of biological processes such as birth, growth, ageing, death and sex, or from the ordinary experience of family life, politics, artistic creation or craftsmanship. He classified metaphysics, therefore, as either 'biomorphic' or 'sociomorphic' or 'technomorphic'. Having done this, he was content to conclude that metaphysics is a redundant duplication of the ordinary and familiar activities or experiences on which it is modelled. The metaphysical doctrines appear, on this argument, as substitutions – and superfluous ones at that – for the original models. On the present argument, Topitsch's observation that mythology and metaphysics are 'derived' from ordinary and familiar experience is perfectly correct. But Topitsch, it would seem, is wrong in his conclusion that mythology and metaphysics are nothing but an unnecessary substitution for these experiences. It seems, on the contrary that the typological elaboration of the ordinary, initial experience, is highly necessary. For that experience functions symbolically to define feeling-states – that is, it is the objective correlative of feeling-states. This is not to claim that ordinary experience is something other than it is. It is, however, also what it *appears* to be, i.e., a symbol. And as a symbol, it requires elaboration and, what is more, typological elaboration. And it is for this reason that we obtain mythology and, eventually, metaphysics. Topitsch, by confining his attention to the very obvious isomorphism of metaphysics (and mythology) and ordinary social, artistic or biological events, jumped to the wrong conclusion. Had he examined the intervening typological elaboration more carefully, he would not have been able to conclude that metaphysics is a redundant duplication of ordinary experience. This criticism of Topitsch's conclusion does not invalidate his initial insight nor his classification of metaphysical doctrines as either biomorphic or technomorphic or sociomorphic. On the contrary: it subscribes to the insight and to the classification but questions the conclusion which Topitsch has drawn from it. In view of these recent, widely discussed examples, it would be wrong to dismiss the substitution theories as the products of an age of positivistic rationalism, now passed. If the confusion underlying substitution theories is allowed to prevail, it becomes imperative to attempt to reduce each myth or metaphor to the things it is supposed (mistakenly) to stand for. Solar deities are regarded as substitutes for the sun and attempts are made to unveil myths and metaphors to find out what they *really* mean. There remains, in such cases, always the problem why a substitution was invented in the first place and why people could not get themselves to call a spade a spade and why, instead of looking at the sun, they had to embroider the image of the sun until it assumed the shape of a deity. One of the most plausible theories to account for the refusal and reluctance to call a spade a spade is the theory that primitive people must have found it difficult to do this because they were untutored and pre-logical in their thinking. But this theory becomes much less plausible when we recall that Malinowski stressed very emphatically that the Trobriand islanders knew perfectly well where babies come from and that one should not take their mythology about procreation at its face value as an indication of their ignorance. H. Werner wrote that close and precise knowledge of the hard facts of life is for primitive people with a narrow subsistence margin a necessary condition for survival.[3] It would seem, therefore, that primitive people cannot really afford metaphors and that if they *do* indulge in them it is not because of ignorance of what the world is *really* like. Hence it is not very credible that the refusal to call a spade a spade stems from lack of intelligence.

These substitution theories have a time-honoured ancestry. Over a century ago Max Müller, the most flamboyant of all nineteenth-century philologists, advanced a theory that mythology is a disease of language. He tried to show that the rays of the sun can become the fingers of God; rain-clouds, heavenly cows with full udders; a medicine-man, Zeus. Andrew Lang contradicted the philological evidence offered by Müller in support of these confusions and argued that the confusions were psychological rather than philological. But he too agreed that myths originated because primitive people kept substituting untruths for truth, udders for clouds and Zeus for medicine-men. In fairness to both Müller and Lang, one has to admit that they put their finger on an important point. They saw clearly that myth is a form of metaphor. Rain-clouds and udders are thrown together, some of their features detached from the place they occupy in nature and so one gets an entirely new image. It does not really matter to us now whether the error is psychological in the sense that the mixing of elements is due to a belief that material events are animistic or whether it is due to a disease of language and derives from philological confusions. What really matters is that both Lang and Müller drew a mistaken inference from their observation that myth is metaphor. They were both unaware that feeling-states cannot be described literally and that symbolisation is not an extravagant and expendable luxury. They believed that symbols and their elaborations by typologically related metaphors are unnecessary and superfluous. Hence they saw the symbol and its metaphorical elaboration as an error of thought through which something untrue (a heavenly cow) had been substituted for something true (rain-clouds). They argued that one can arrive at the truth if one gives up the redundant and erroneous duplicate and looks instead at the event it signifies. Again we find that the initial observation that myth is metaphor is right;

75

but that the inference that metaphors are superfluous is wrong. Müller and Lang belong to the past but their mistake is being repeated time and time over by Allegro and Swanson, Graves and Topitsch, none of whom have any newer theory about the refusal to call a spade a spade. None of them can answer the crucial question why people should make the mistake, and make it so ubiquitously and so persistently, of substituting a cross for a mushroom, an udder for a cloud, a spiritual being for a political constitution. The only plausible answer is that the substitution is not a mistake but a mental and intellectual necessity forced upon man by the inability to describe a feeling-state literally. And, moreover, that the substitution is not in fact a substitution but an elaboration. The udder is not a sign for the rain-cloud; but an anti-type of the rain cloud.

There remains the possibility, advocated by the so-called Myth and Ritual School, that the refusal to call a spade a spade is due to the fact that myths are explanations of ritual. This theory maintains that the ancient Greeks did not in fact substitute the God Helios for the sun. They argue instead that there was an ancient ritual in which a priest named Helios drove a chariot and that the myth about Helios the sun-god was invented to explain the performance of the ritual. Hence there was no refusal to call a spade a spade and the myth emerged as an explanation of a ritual performance.

Whatever the plausibility of this theory, it does not really solve our substitution problem, for it merely pushes the problem one stage further back. Even if one were to grant that myths originated as explanations of rituals – and there are many good reasons for granting this at least in some cases – the refusal to call a spade a spade is not explained. The myth may not be a substitution for an ordinary experience but an explanation of a rite. But then we are left with the question: why the rite? Any ritual is a formalisation of an ordinary activity and stands to that ordinary activity in exactly the same typological relationship in which a myth stands to a story or recital of an ordinary event. If we consider that myths, or at least some myths, are explanations of rites rather than substitutions for ordinary events, we are left with the question why the rite in question was substituted for the ordinary activity. For example, why was the slaughter of a sheep for food replaced by the ritual killing of a ram for sacrificial purposes? The Myth and Ritual School may be able to account for the existence of myths or for the existence of some myths. But it cannot account for the existence of ritual without invoking the simple substitution theory. If the advocates of a simple substitution theory have to postulate that myths originate because primitive people cannot call a spade a spade, the adherents of the Myth and Ritual School have to postulate that primitive people substitute rites for ordinary performances because they are too simple-minded to *use* a spade as a spade. The argument that ritual is prior to myth may explain myths, but it does not offer a solution of the problem why substitutions should take place. For this reason we must conclude that the Myth and Ritual School, whatever its merits, like the straight substitution theories, has to fall back upon the notion that primitive people are not observant and are unable to reason clearly. And, as stated above, there is no good argument for believing that this is so. If we recognise, as I have argued all along, that symbols are *not* redundant substitutes for natural events and that natural events themselves are often used as symbols (i.e., that they are used not for what they are but for how they *appear* to be) and that the sum total of natural events has to be supplemented by the creation of additional events through the method of metaphor because natural events, though symbols, are poor and inadequate symbols – if all this is recognised, the need for all theories to account for substitution disappears.

The Myth and Ritual School hoped to account for the fact that myths are usually 'tall stories', that is, stories which cannot possibly be believed to have happened. By explaining the myth as a story told to explain a ritual they hoped to account for its 'tallness'. The theory appeared in a strong and a weak form. In its strong form it was first put forward by K. O. Müller in 1825. Then Usener used it to explain the origins of the names of gods and eventually revived as a *tour de force* by Lord Raglan's contention that there is only one single original ritual, the annual slaying and replacing of a king. In this strong form it is diffusionist and holds that all other rituals and myths are derived from it by diffusion. In its weaker form it merely asserts that myths arise from rituals in the sense that myths are ritual-bound tales which have a ritual origin or, as Miss Harrison put it, that myth is the spoken correlative of the thing done, the *legomena* which accompany the *drōmena*. In its weaker form it is not diffusion-ist and can be applied to any myth and ritual. In its weaker form, the theory may be true enough, but it does not explain anything at all.

For we are still left with the ritual. Why should people substitute a ritual slaying for an ordinary murder or slaughter, a ritual ablution for the washing of hands for hygienic purposes? The main argument against the Myth and Ritual theory in its weaker form is its lack of explanatory value. There seems no advantage in insisting that there are some rituals which are based on myths and that the theory that myths are always based on rituals must therefore be false.[4] The Christian Mass is cited as one such ritual. But if anything, this example merely confirms that all myths come in typological series. The Mass is admittedly a ritual based on a myth. The myth, in turn, is an assimilation of a historical event (or presumably historical event) to a prior ritual, the common repast. The mythicised historical event is a step in a long series, and the Mass is a ritual which is yet another, further specified step in the same series.

Once the proper role of symbols, be they natural events or re-shuffled natural events (i.e., myths and metaphors), is understood, it becomes clear that a myth or a metaphor does not stand for a natural event; but that the natural event is itself the first link in the typological series. On this assumption, the sun as a natural phenomenon is a symbol (among other things), and the solar deity is a further symbol, that is, an anti-type of the type. But it does not stand for the sun and is not a substitute for the sun. Similarly, God is not a father-figure. But a father may be considered as a symbol and then be elaborated and embroidered into a metaphor and myth by being turned into God. God does not stand for father anymore than father stands for God. The symbol, that is, an event or its elaboration by way of metaphor or formalisation, cannot be reduced to anything *other* than itself. It is what it is. The situation is asymmetrical. An event or object is both itself and something other, e.g., a symbol. But a symbol is what it is and it cannot be dissolved or reduced to what it means. It symbolises a feeling-state. If one wishes one can say that it means that feeling-state. But there is little gain in this formulation since the feeling-state as it stands (i.e. unsymbolised) is ineffable and incapable of literal description. A symbol can therefore not be said to mean what could be described literally. A symbol can therefore never become redundant or superfluous. A sign is redundant as soon as one can produce the thing it stands for. But a symbol cannot become thus redundant, because one cannot produce the feeling-state. If one could give a literal description of the feeling-state, the symbol

would be a mere sign and could conceivably become superfluous –
an unnecessary duplication. This way of looking at the matter was
the core of a great debate on literary criticism which aroused much
heat in France. Owing to the habit of intellectual abstraction so
prevalent in French thought and owing to the fact that the debate
centred on a question of purely literary criticism, its importance was
not readily appreciated outside France. Roughly speaking, Picard
maintained that a work of literature is a sign and Barthes that it is a
symbol.[5] The rights and wrongs of the debate must depend, of course,
on the works considered and this simple possibility of a solution was
obscured by the high level of abstraction employed by the partici-
pants. But the crux of the matter is that as far as myths and certain
works literary, though admittedly not all, are concerned, Barthes's
contention is correct. Camus's *L'Étranger* is *la façon d'exister d'un
silence* and not a book *about* a crime and a trial. The book as it
stands is a symbol. It is not a symbol of silence but a way of silent
existence which symbolises an otherwise quite ineffable state of consciousness or mind. The symbol reveals its meaning as part of a
typological series if and only if one can gauge the specification
towards which the series tends. This is completely disregarded and
overlooked by all the above-discussed substitution theories. These
theories assume that a symbol is nothing more than a sign and that
one can gauge its meaning by replacing it by the things signified.
The only question of interpretation which arises on this assumption
is to discover the thing it signifies. In fairness one should add that the
mistake of the theory was not prompted by an inability to distinguish
between sign and symbol. That distinction is obvious enough. The
temptation to overlook and obscure it and, in fact, deny it, derived,
on the contrary, from the desire to interpret. In the absence of a
proper appreciation of the role of typology, the temptation to confuse
sign and symbol became irresistible because, once made, it offered
a simple and naïve method of interpretation. The appreciation of
typology and the possibility of an alternative interpretation offered
by it will help to confirm the important distinction between sign
and symbol.

TEN

SYMBOLS AND PSYCHOLOGY

The distinction between symbol and sign is particularly relevant to the importance attributed to mythology in many modern psychological theories. In most of these theories it is assumed that myths and metaphors are substitutes of, or stand for, ordinary natural events the knowledge of which is, for some reason or other, supposed to be repressed. As a form of pragmatic therapy, this way of looking at the matter may have its merits. If one can untie a neurosis by persuading a man that his fear of God, which prevents him from loving his children or holding down a job, is nothing but a fear of his father, one has obviously rendered him a service. But philosophically speaking, there is no justification for this form of argument. For the father, though a natural phenomenon, is just as much a symbol as God. It is less embroidered and therefore less specific; and, therefore, typologically, lower in the series. But it is nevertheless just as much a symbol as God. This contention is based upon the reflection that, in the first instance, symbols are culled from the natural world we live in; and that myth and metaphors are only extended and re-shuffled symbols, the elements of which are derived from the natural world. The whole body of psychological interpretations which insist on the idea that symbols are symbols of natural events or experiences which we do not allow ourselves to face or speak about must therefore be relegated to the realm of pragmatic therapy; but should not be considered as a possible method of understanding the meaning of mythology. The open approach to mythical imagery here proposed rests on the symbolic equivalence of the natural event seized as a symbol and the metaphoric image constructed from the convergence of several natural events. Equivalence does not, of course imply that the two kinds of symbols (natural event and metaphor) are equidistant from the feeling-state that is symbolised. On the contrary, the typologically developed metaphor is more exact in its symbolisation and therefore less distant. But the contention that there is symbolical equivalence between natural event and metaphor excludes the techniques of interpretation developed by psychiatry from consideration in the present context. In psychotherapy a symbol represents a natural event which has been repressed. For reasons of efficiency, therapeutic techniques distinguish the symbol that is taken by the patient to *represent* the repressed object. In neither case is it admitted that the symbol and the object it is or represents are symbolically equivalent in that both symbolise a feeling-state. In consequence of this psychotherapeutic postulate, the various psychiatric methods of interpreting mythology are not surveyed here. This is not to be taken as a criticism of any of these methods. If the therapist derives practical help from the postulate in his effort to cure patients, the postulate has a pragmatic justification of which the psychotherapist and the patient must be the best judges. But when one's interest is not centred on patients who suffer but on the mythologies of people who are healthy, a completely different perspective is called for.

Although we omit psychiatric interpretations of symbols from consideration because of the assumption underlying psychiatric practice that the reshuffled symbol symbolises the natural event and the implied *rejection* of the idea that the natural event is itself a symbol, albeit a not very specific one, we might in passing wonder whether psychiatric thought could not benefit from a revision of this assumption which is so greatly dependent on nineteenth-century positivism. The assumption, positivistically, states that natural events are the events that really happen and that some people for a variety of reasons either distort and embroider them or repress or sublimate them, thus departing from reality by creating illusion or false consciousness. In this sense, Max Müller's renowned and by now completely outmoded interpretations of mythic images as unwarranted personifications of or substitutions for natural and cosmic events are all of a piece with the by no means outmoded hermeneutics of Freud and all post-Freudians, orthodox as well as revisionist. The latter would be very shocked to realise that methodologically they have not advanced beyond Max Müller who, in spite of his enormous philological learning, appears nowadays as a slightly comic figure.

Let us consider an example. There is a widely discussed psychiatric theory which states that schizoid behaviour, and possibly schizophrenia, are caused by a 'double bind'. A double bind situation is a situation in which a person, no matter how he reacts, cannot win. A foolproof situation is one in which not even a fool can go wrong. A double bind is a little like a saneproof situation. A saneproof situation is one in which not even a sane person can go right. According to the theory that the double bind causes schizoid behaviour, a person who is simultaneously exposed to stimulation and frustration or to rapidly alternating stimulation and frustration[1] will eventually develop schizoid behaviour. In this view, the initial state of the double bind is the hard natural event which *causes* schizoid behaviour. The person exposed to the double bind, for instance, might end up by feeling that he is split into a mind and a body, incapable of integration. This split involves usually an identification with the mind and an alienation from the body.[2] Since the split is a response to the double bind and thus caused by it, it follows that the split occurs because the patient is unable to tolerate the double bind. The split is therefore a substitute for the double bind and must be considered its symbol. If the patient had been able to stand the double bind – and many hardy people can stand this particular and many other double binds – there would have been no need for substitute behaviour.

Suppose we try to revise this whole conceptual frame. Let us assume that the double bind itself is the first attempt to symbolise a state of mind. This view is quite plausible, for although double bind situations are almost universal, only very few people fasten their attention on them. This shows that although the symbol (in this case the natural event of a double bind) is available in almost every family, only few people use it as a symbol because only to those few people is it an adequate expression of their state of mind or their feeling-states. Most other people pass it by or shrug it off. If, however, it is seized as a symbol, its inadequacy and imprecision, that is, the poverty effect, is soon discovered. Then follows the next step. A re-shuffling takes place. The original situation is embroidered and mythologised and next we get behaviour which reflects this mythologisation. The person in question no longer sees himself in a double bind but sees himself split into a body and a mind, incapable of connecting the one with the other. There is a clear typological relation between the natural event (the double bind) and the mythological situation. The first is the type; the second, the anti-type. The two symbols are ontologically equivalent. But the more specific anti-type is a more appropriate and precise symbol than the less specific type. At the same time, the abundance effect comes into operation. For the person concerned need not necessarily specify the type-symbol (the double bind) by the anti-type of the split or of this particular kind of split between body and mind. Other possibilities have been observed. The main point, however, is that there is no 'causal' relationship between the two symbols. One should not say that the split is the symbol of the double bind and that the double bind 'causes' the split because the double bind is intolerable and therefore has to be substituted by the split. Similarly one should not think of the double bind situation as *real* and of the split as an illusion, for there are many people who are in a double bind but, since they find it tolerable, make nothing of it. For these people it is hardly 'real'. But if one says that the natural event, the double bind, is a symbol of a feeling-state, one can see the split as a more advanced form of symbolisation. The pursuit of the more specific symbol has then more to recommend itself than avoidance of the less specific symbol. Any person to whom the double bind is a meaningful symbol will be greatly tempted to elaborate it typologically into the latter. So far, not only is there no harm done, but elaboration is a gain in clarity. The poverty effect has been neutralised and, if anything, been replaced by the abundance effect: the person can now freely choose which kind of elaboration he wishes to use and he can even decide to use now one and now another elaboration. The real harm begins when symbolisation becomes addictive and the person ceases to be free to seek further elaboration of the symbol or not to seek it, ceases to be able to avail himself freely of the abundance effect, and remains saddled with one particular, compulsive, elaboration. When a person begins to be *compelled* to symbolise a feeling-state by dwelling on the double bind, mental disturbance sets in. This mental disturbance is the addiction to the double bind symbol. It is not the double bind as a natural event. And when, next, a typological transformation of the original situation, conceived as a symbol, takes place in order to eliminate the poverty effect and when the addiction to the first symbol is transmitted, as it is very likely to be, to the elaborated symbol (i.e. the split), the mental illness is well under way.

Although the double bind theory is an example from very recent psychiatric thought, the same argument can be applied, *mutatis mutandis*, to every time-honoured textbook example of penis envy or Oedipal desire. The established conceptual framework has it that the penis envy is a natural event which is suppressed and replaced by, for example, a hysterical paralysis of the legs. Since the repression necessitates substitution, the hysterical paralysis is looked upon as a symbol of the penis envy and the penis envy is the natural fact. When it is admitted consciously and faced up to, it is genuine consciousness or reality; when it is suppressed and symbolised as hysterical paralysis, there is 'false consciousness'. According to the proposed revision, penis envy should be considered as the first, fairly unspecified symbol of a state of mind. And the hysterical paralysis should be considered as a typological elaboration of the initial symbol. Or consider another example. According to the customary and conventional way of thinking, when some people's emotional life becomes fixated upon anal pleasure, they will become miserly, greedy and ungenerous. It is alleged that anality causes greed and that greed is a symbol for anality. Greed is substituted for anality. Anality is the fact; and greed a disguise of a fact. The substitution of a symbol for what is alleged to be a fact results in the creation of false consciousness. When people are greedy, they deceive themselves and ought to learn or be made to learn to look the truth in the face, that is, they ought to learn to accept their own anality. In the revised scheme it is proposed that both anal pleasure and greed are considered as symbols of one and the same state of mind. There are two symbols: anality and greed. The one expresses the state of mind less clearly than the other. Both symbols are typologically related in that they elaborate the *typos* of retention or retentiveness; but one is more specific than the other. The substitution of the one for the other does not occur because, for some reason or other, people seek to create a false consciousness and deceive themselves and hide the truth from themselves (repression); but because they elaborate the symbolic image in order to achieve more specification and clarity.

The proposed, revised, scheme amounts to no more and no less than the abandonment of the concept of repression. Instead, it is proposed that we replace it by looking at the thing repressed as well as at the substituted image as typologically related symbols of one and the same state of mind. The substitution occurs not because we seek to repress, but because we seek further clarification of our state of mind. Hence the increased specification in the substitute symbol. The proposed revision may appear outrageous. But when one considers that there is no direct evidence for repression; and that in the nature of the case there cannot be any direct evidence for repression; and that the notion of repression was arrived at by inference because it was noticed that people did substitute, for example, greed for anal pleasure, there will be nothing shocking in the proposal. There is no independent evidence that repression takes place. Repression was postulated because substitutions were observed. But if one manages to explain substitutions as progressive typological elaborations, the need for the postulate of repression disappears.

It is not immediately obvious whether the proposed revision of concepts will result in a practical therapeutic advantage or not. In the old scheme, a girl who suffers from penis envy, but finds it tolerable, is not driven to further symbolisation. She does not repress the true and real consciousness and substitute a false consciousness for it. In the new scheme, a person who finds penis envy tolerable willl not dwell on it and designate it as a symbol. In either scheme there is no explanation why some people mind, and why others do not mind, penis envy. The only genuine advantage of the new scheme is that it avoids the apparently completely arbitrary definition of not minding penis envy as a sense of *reality*; and the consequent, equally arbitrary definition of the symbolic substitute as *illusion*. In the new scheme, there is neither a sense of reality nor an illusion, but both the natural event and the elaborated symbol are considered ontologically equivalent. In the new scheme, the absence of an arbitrary definition of reality is more realistic. By implication, in the new scheme, the concept of repression disappears and is replaced by the phenomenon of typological elaboration.

If one pursues this line of reasoning a little further, one will arrive at the conclusion that the important distinction is not between feelings that are conscious and feelings that are unconscious or repressed. The distinction is valid, but seems less fundamental than is commonly supposed. The really important distinction is between those feeling-states that are inchoate because they have not yet been symbolised and those that have already been symbolised. The former cannot be referred to at all as they stand. The latter can be referred to literally – the literal reference being precisely to the symbol and not the state of feeling. In the latter case the reference is a sign of the symbol and can be substituted for it; but in the former case no reference is possible until a symbol has been designated. It is possible that this distinction between unreferrable feelings and feelings that can be referred to and the references to which can be described literally runs parallel to the distinction between conscious and unconscious feelings and that one means by the second distinction the first distinction.

One could even throw out the suggestion, although this can be considered no more than a suggestion, that the revised conceptual framework of psychiatric thought may throw some light on the vexed question of the biochemical conditioning of mental illness. If the revised conceptual framework is accepted, one could say that the whole process of symbolisation is a perfectly natural function of the mind. First it is found that the double bind situation is a meaningful symbol for a certain person; and then it is discovered that a typological elaboration of the first symbol is desirable and even more meaningful. According to this new way of looking at it the situation becomes pathological when there is addiction and compulsion – that is, addiction to a certain symbol rather than to another, and compulsion to symbolise, rather than toy with symbolisation or pass the possibility up altogether. Hence we might think that if there is biochemical malfunctioning at the basis of pathology, it has nothing to do with symbolisation but that it has something to do with the addiction and the compulsion. If this is true, it would follow that any biochemical malfunctioning has nothing to do with any specific imagery which is used by the patient. There is, for example, nothing specially biochemical in whether a person thinks he is Napoleon or whether he imagines he is being persecuted by clocks. The biochemical malfunctioning involved relates purely to the addictiveness and the compulsion.

However this may be, it is interesting to note that while most contemporary psychologists and psychoanalysts keep adhering to the old mechanical conceptual framework in which certain natural events are repressed and then re-emerge as symbols, Freud himself had an inkling of the importance of the revised scheme here proposed. To begin with he used to believe that the tales or fantasies of adult hysterics were fictions or symbols which arose from memory traces of traumas suffered in early childhood. This way of looking at the psychogenesis of mental illness is in accord with the old mechanical conceptual framework according to which illness results from the substitution of fantasies or symbols for repressed *real* experiences. These symbols stand for the facts. But in the late nineties of the last century, it began to dawn on Freud that in many cases the alleged childhood traumas had never really occurred at all. As he wrote to his friend Fliess, when he played cards with the father of one of his women patients he kept wondering why so nice an old gentleman should or could ever have attempted to rape his infant daughter whom Freud was now treating, as an adult, for hysterical complaints. But then it struck him more and more forcefully that the attempted rape had never occurred and that it was merely a wish to which the woman patient had become addicted. He then began to conclude that the traumas are no more real than the symbols and that the symbol (the hysterical symptom) was not a substitute for repressed trauma, such as a rape attempted by the father; but was just as fictitious an image as the trauma itself. In this way Freud came very near to spotting the ontological equivalence of all symbols and to discovering that the attempted rape was an image of a state of feeling and that the subsequently developed hysterical symptom was *not* caused by the original image; but was a typological elaboration of the earlier image and that the one as well as the other *stood* for or meant one and the same state of mind or feeling. One can take it that this was indeed the implication of his discovery that hysteria can be due to incest fantasy as much as to actual incest or actually attempted incest. The outcome of this insight is that a fantasy and an actual occurrence, as images, are symbolically equivalent. Freud, however, was prevented from ever clearly formulating the consequences of his own discovery because he was not able to wean himself from the mechanical conception that symbols (in this case, hysteria) symbolise actual occurrences. All he could therefore conclude from his insight was that the symbol symbolised either actual incest or an incest fantasy. He was precluded by his own mechanistic framework from working forward to the idea that both the actual occurrence and the fantasy were symbols too; and that the hysteria was a further, more specified extension of the other symbols.

In some way, Freud remained a prisoner of his own mechanistic philosophy of causation. When he considered the matter, he tried to reformulate the principle of mechanical causation; but failed, because he could not elaborate an alternative vocabulary. Thus he wrote for instance in *Studies on Hysteria*[3] that the principal feature of the genesis of neuroses is that they are, as a rule, overdetermined – that several factors come together to produce the result. The notion of 'overdetermination' was clearly an attempt to formulate something approaching the preceding argument in terms of the old view of causal determination. The notion 'overdetermination', in strict mechanical causation principles, makes no sense at all. But it took many decades before Harry Guntrip was able to write: 'the upshot is that the terms of physical science and the physical cause-and-effect type of explanation are not relevant or suitable to psychic phenomena. Psychoanalysis provides a new model for personality as a complex of various psychic levels and structures that enables the phenomena of personal living – i.e. those of conscious and unconscious conflict – to be explained on the basis of overdetermination and plurality of causes, "cause" being no longer understood in the physical sense.'[4] The present proposal amounts to no more than a final conclusion to Guntrip's argument. It is a proposal to drop the vocabulary of causation altogether and thus avoid the concept of overdetermination and replace it by the view that both the causes of neuroses and the neurotic results are typologically related symbols which *mean* one and the same state of mind.

There are and probably always have been two powerful and apparently contradictory movements of thought about symbols. On one side there is the tendency to de-mystify symbolic discourse, to strip symbols of their appearance and uncover the meaning they seek to hide. This tendency seeks to discover the reality that is hidden behind the illusion created by the symbol. On the other side there is the tendency to re-mythicise discourse and to restore meaning to everyday language, common-sense perception and utilitarian activity. In both cases the activity is hermeneutic. There is an attempt to decipher. In the one case we attempt to decipher symbols; and in the other, ordinary events. If one takes a closer look at these two tendencies, one will find that the contradiction is in appearance only. If one says, as Paul Ricoeur does,[5] that the one tendency seeks to restore the *logos* behind the *mythos* and the other the *mythos* behind the *logos*, the two goals are seemingly opposed to each other. But it all depends in which direction one is reading the typological series. If one reads it in a forward direction and proceeds from natural events towards metaphysical abstraction or covers any one segment of the series in forward direction one can think of finding the *logos* behind the *mythos* and uncover step by step the veil of poetry which progressive specified symbolisation casts over the less specified symbols and, eventually, over the natural event. If one reads the series backwards and starts with the metaphysical abstraction and seeks out the light which that abstraction casts upon every less specified symbol in a downward direction, one is restoring the *mythos* to the *logos*. In this case, one is reading nature in the light of poetry or metaphysics.

Consider a concrete example. If one is working one's way upwards towards greater specification one starts with the phallus, then finds a tree and eventually, even more specified, a cathedral spire. Looking forward from the natural object (phallus) towards the more highly specified symbol (cathedral spire) one will find that the more specified symbol hides the less specified, and creates, if one likes to use the term, an illusion. The illusion disguises something and if one wants to tear away illusion, one must reach back to the natural object it hides. This way lies truth. If one is working downwards, however, one will start with the cathedral spire and look, first, towards the tree and eventually contemplate the phallus. At first, the tree is seen in the light the cathedral spire throws on it, and finally, the phallus, in the light both cathedral spire and tree throw on it. Working in this way, one arrives at truth by reading the phallus in the light of cathedral spires and one is restoring meaning to a natural object by using a highly specified symbol as a stencil that is superimposed upon the natural object.

The lesson to be learnt from this example is plain. The cathedral spire symbol conceals and reveals, disguises and discloses at one and the same time. Whether it does the one or the other depends entirely on the direction in which one is moving. In one sense it conceals the phallus and the discovery that the phallus stands serially behind the cathedral spire, reveals a truth. In the other sense, the cathedral spire reveals the phallus in a special light and the discovery that the phallus, among other meanings, means a cathedral spire, or can be seen as an unspecified and roughly hewn cathedral spire, teaches us a truth about the phallus which was hidden as long as the phallus is contemplated as a natural object. I would imagine that the effectiveness of William Golding's novel *The Spire* depends precisely on this ambivalence of its central symbol. If one traces the typological series forward, the spire conceals and hides the phallus. If one traces the same series backwards, the spire reveals something about the phallus. Reality and illusion, true and false consciousness are available all along the series. Every one term of the series both discloses and disguises at one and the same time. If one comes from the specified top and looks down to the unspecified bottom, every term discloses something. If one comes from the bottom and looks upwards towards the specified top, every term disguises something. If one takes the bottom as one's fixed and starting point and moves upwards, one will get a thickening veil, a sense of growing illusion because the original starting point disappears from sight. If one takes the top of the series as one's fixed starting point and moves downwards, one will find that the bottom of the series appears to have a specific meaning bestowed by the abstract top. If one starts at the bottom, man is the reality and the image of God is fashioned in the image of man. If one starts at the top, God is the reality and one will finally see man made in the image of God. Which is truth and which is illusion depends on the direction in which one is traversing the typological series. Taking the spire as a half-way mark in a typological series one can interpret it either as disguising something or as disclosing something. If one comes from the bottom it disguises something. If one comes from the top, it discloses something. The activity of interpretation (hermeneutics) is therefore not an absolute activity which under all circumstances reveals the truth behind an illusion. Coming from the bottom, it reveals a truth behind an illusion; and coming from the top, it reveals an illusion behind a truth. If one looks at the phallus in cold blood, the substitution of the cathedral spire is an attempt to disguise something, to 'repress' the phallus, to avoid calling something by its proper name. But coming from the top, the substitution of the phallus for the cathedral spire shows that the phallus is not what it is when contemplated in cold blood but that it has a meaning which it derives from the spire. Travelling in either direction, we are interpreting. Travelling upwards we are destroying the illusion that a spire is a spire. Travelling downwards, we are destroying the illusion that a phallus is a phallus. The crux of the matter is that the series phallus–tree–spire is not just a series of isomorphic images. It is a series with a sense of direction which proceeds from a natural object which is unspecific to greater and greater levels of specification. Hence we can think of traversing the series upwards or downwards. Hence the difference in the results of interpretation, according to the direction in which we are traversing the series. If the images were simply isomorphic and if there were no progressive specifications in the images, one could not establish a sense of direction and this kind of interpretation would be impossible.

There is a practical irony. If one wants to move upwards and interpret the spire as a disguise of the reality, of the phallus, one must, for convenience sake, start with the spire. Obviously, the disguise precedes, in the order of perception or awareness, the disguised reality. So in order to move upwards, one has to start at the top and peel away the several layers of disguise. But the opposite does not hold. If one wants to interpret the phallus in the light of the spire and move downwards, one must in fact move downwards and start with the truth of the spire and let it shed its light upon the world of less specified objects. For practical purposes therefore, though not in our logical understanding of the processes of interpretation, the movement is downwards in both cases. But this must not blind us to the fact that in the first case one is logically moving upwards and taking the spire as disguising something that ought to be laid bare; and that in the second case one is moving downwards both logically and practically by taking the spire as something that discloses something that has to be seen in the light shed upon it.

ELEVEN

THE TRUTH VALUE OF SYMBOLS

There is one thing structuralists and functionalists have in common. They can both afford to disregard the question whether myths are true or in what sense they are true. The whole question, which has troubled men for millennia, whether God really exists or whether He can be re-incarnated and resurrected or whether God is real and Zeus is not, is of no concern to functionalists and structuralists. The one examines the function of myth in a given social order; the other considers the manner in which myth resolves incomprehensible contradictions inherent in any social order. The question as to the truth value of myth does not arise. As soon as one eschews both functionalism and structuralism, the old question as to the truth of the myths is bound to re-appear. It is perfectly true that the sophisticated man of the twentieth century feels a bit sheepish in debating the question whether God exists, although he has been found from time to time to do precisely this just as his ancestors were wont to do. But the very people who proclaim a sort of unconcern in this age-old question as to the truth of myth rightly have no hesitation in discussing why the Nuer think that birds are twins and what they could mean when they say something which is zoologically patently untrue.[1] It was probably one of the tacit attractions of both structuralism and functionalism that they by-passed this vexed question. It may count against the revival of typology that it forces it once again into the centre of the picture. At the same time, it seems that that account of metaphor and symbol may contribute something towards a solution of this question and make it less vexed. The contention that there is a symbolic equivalence of the natural event functioning as a symbol and the metaphorical images which help to specify it typologically has an important consequence. Even though this equivalence does not imply and in fact excludes, equidistance of all symbols from states of feeling, it has the effect of removing the difference between the ontological status of the natural event and the metaphorical image. As symbols, both images, the image of the natural event and the metaphorical, constructed, image, are equivalent. The natural event can be located in space and time by its relationship to other events. It is part of nature and is functionally related to other parts of nature in the manner in which the world of nature was characterised above. But when a natural event is used as a symbol, this relationship to other natural events and its ontological status as part of natural reality ceases to be important or of any consequence. It then becomes, like the constructed metaphorical image, an object of contemplation. 'Imagination', Collingwood wrote in *The Principles of Art,* 'is indifferent to the distinction between the real and the unreal.'[2] The aesthetic consciousness, Cassirer argued, leaves the problem whether its objects really exist or not behind.[3] The image, Herbert Read comments, exists in its own right and in its presentational immediacy. It is received and felt, a moment of original vision and an intuitive extension of consciousness.[4] And, again, Michael Oakeshott: 'Where imagining is "contemplating", fact and not-fact do not appear.'[5] When images are seized as symbols it does not matter whether they are taken straight from nature or whether they are metaphorical compositions. The difference between illusion and reality disappears. The symbols *qua* symbols are all ontologically equivalent.

One might argue that the acceptance of such a view entails an elimination of our power to distinguish between mirage and reality and hence between sanity and insanity or hallucination. There is admittedly a certain difficulty here. William Golding in *Lord of the Flies* makes a poignant comment. The stranded children are terrified by the appearance of a billowing white object behind a hill. But some of them are rational and explore and detect that the billowing object is only a parachute blown up by the wind and attached to a pilot's corpse. Here there was clear survival value in the ability to distinguish an image which was a mirage from an image which was a reality; to distinguish between illusion and reality and to be able to assign definite ontological status to the billowing parachute and deprive the white billowing object that looked like a breathing ghost of its ontological status and declare it to have been an illusion. But fortunately we are not always faced with such extreme need for sheer survival. And in situations of more urbane human comfort, there is great merit in effacing the distinction and in believing that symbols are ontologically equivalent. As far as the implications for our ability to distinguish sanity from insanity are concerned, the obliteration of the difference between symbols which are facts and symbols which are metaphors is unimportant. For it is quite wrong to define sanity as a sense of reality and equate it with the state in which a person does not imagine that he is Napoleon. We all, from time to time, imagine that we are Napoleon and such imagining does not make us insane. The hallmark of sanity lies in the ability to stop imagining that one is Napoleon; not in the fact that one sometimes daydreams that one is. Sanity, therefore, is not to be defined by a person's adherence to a predefined picture of reality and insanity by a refusal or inability to so adhere. The difference between sanity and insanity consists in the degree of compulsiveness or obsessiveness with which a person adheres to certain imaginings. If the freedom to change imaginings and to substitute one for another is lost, sanity is threatened. But as long as freedom is preserved, the mere fact of daydreaming (or, for that matter, of night-dreaming) is of no importance. If this is granted and if it is accepted that sanity is constituted by compulsiveness rather than by a lack of a sense of predefined reality, the theory of symbolical equivalence neither obviates the need to distinguish sanity from madness nor removes our ability to do so.

All the same, the consequences of this proposed revision of current psychological thinking are far-reaching. Ronald Fairbairn in a famous paper[6] stated that the ability to discriminate between the inner and outer world is an important function of the ego and added that failure to distinguish is a schizoid phenomenon and indicates a weak ego formation. If the present revision were accepted, one could no longer argue that failure to distinguish between an inner and an outer world is schizoid. On the contrary, one would have to recognise such a failure as nothing more than the result of typological elaborations of symbolic images, and consider instead the compulsive addiction to any one of these images, be they culled from the inner world or the outer world, as a criterion of insanity or, at least, as a schizoid phenomenon. The splitting of the ego which is of the essence of schizophrenia would then not stem from a failure to distinguish but from the compulsive accretion of ego-consciousness around any one particular image.

The theory of the symbolic equivalence of images regardless of their ontological status gains added strength when one considers how arbitrary all attempts to distinguish the ontological status of one image from that of another really are. One is very hard put to state the difference in status between a dream and a daydream; between a dream and an imaginary image. The distinction between a hope and a memory may be somewhat easier; but we know that so many hopes are really projected memories (if one looks at their psychogenesis) that even here the distinction seems unstable. Both in antiquity and in the middle ages, people seemed to have no difficulty in believing that some mythical images have a status of actual reality in a world other than the natural world perceived by our senses. For simplicity's sake the medieval schoolmen called that world the world of super-nature. But here again the distinction between what happens in nature (e.g. the image of a tree, a dream of a tree) and what happens in the world of supernature (God's creation of a tree) seems arbitrary from a distance. For the schoolmen, to a man, were adamant that the images contained in Greek and Roman mythology, though incapable of being assigned a status of reality in the natural world, were nevertheless not to be assigned a status of reality in the world of supernature. In other words, the criterion of distinction which they used to assign reality status in the supernatural world to one set of images, and deny it to another, was not only arbitrary in the sense in which the attempted distinctions between dreams and day-dreams and hopes and memories are; but was also arbitrary in the sense that it was dictated by and dependent on purely ecclesiastico-political circumstances.

One might surmise here something like the possibility of a theory of the relativity of reality. Material events are what they are. Mental events (states of consciousness, feeling-states, etc.), whenever they bring themselves into sharper focus and assume definition, only succeed in doing so by first using material or natural events not for what they are and how they relate themselves to each other but as they appear to feeling-states, that is, as symbols. Next they further succeed with more precision in doing so by bringing about the occur-rence of transformations and metamorphoses of these material events used as symbols. But the ontological status of these symbols and of their metamorphoses of matter varies according to whether it is defined in relation to matter or in relation to mind. When the symbols and metamorphoses are related to matter, it is easy to distinguish between real and imaginary images of matter, between real events and hallucinations, between hallucinations and dreams, and so forth. It is easy so to distinguish because material events relate objectively to other material events and those that do not can be designated as 'imaginary', and imaginary events relate objectively to material events only because their description or pictorial representation do in their capacity as words and pictures.[7] But when the metamorphoses are related to mind, the case is altogether different, for the dualism between mind and matter, between mental and material events, is asymmetrical. Mind, unlike material events, is not self-defining. There is something absolute and final about material events because they stand in fixed relations to one another. The retina is materially related to both the tree and the brain, regardless of whether the tree is seen or whether anyone is conscious of the tree or of seeing the tree. Not so mental events. They assume their shape and definition from the material events that symbolize them. Without the material events and the metamorphoses of these events by which they are rendered more precise, they remain inchoate and unspecific, nebulous and amorphous. They are therefore not final, fixed and absolute, because they cannot be broken up into finite entities that exist in set relationships to one another. If consciousness were to be snuffed out, one could never 'think' of trees ever being seen; but trees would nevertheless continue to stand in certain fixed relationships to retinas or camera lenses and photographic plates and brain cells. But if matter were to be eliminated, consciousness would never again assume specific shapes and definitions. There would be luminosity; but of nothing in particular. Given that the relationship is thus asymmetrical, the definition of the ontological status of the metamorphoses of matter, either really brought about by material combinations (houses, for example, and all material artifacts) or imagined (hallucinations of being chased by lions, giants) or materially depicted imaginings (pictures of giants), is very different when carried out in reference to consciousness. Seeing that consciousness receives its specific and particular shapes from the material events and its various metamorphoses, these events and their metamorphoses cannot be distinguished in their ontological status by reference to consciousness. On the contrary, if one takes mental events as one's starting point and appreciates that they are distinct and specifically distinguishable events *because* they are symbolised or referred to by material events and their metamorphoses, all distinctions between those material events and their many metamorphoses disappear. When one starts with mental events, all these symbols are ontologically equivalent. If one starts with material events, they are not. A bewildering conclusion. A dream and a hallucination (imaginings), a house (constructions), a tree (a natural occurrence) are ontologically equivalent in reference to consciousness and ontologically different in reference to matter. The dualism between mind and matter shows itself to be profoundly asymmetrical.

There are reminiscences and echoes here of phenomenological philosophy. According to phenomenology it is possible to contemplate the phenomena that remain in consciousness after all belief in the existence of the external world is suspended for the time being. It is said that the objects intended by consciousness can be bracketed so that one is left only with their phenomena, i.e. with the objects one is conscious of rather than with the objects themselves. In this case, the objects one is conscious of, the phenomena, will all be of the same status, regardless of whether they are real, hallucinatory, imaginings, dreams or hopes. It is tempting to equate our symbols with the *intentions* of consciousness as phenomenologists are wont to call the objects one is conscious of. But phenomenologists consider the intention to be part and parcel of the occurrence of the mental event (consciousness) and hence they persuade themselves that by focusing one's attention on these intentions, one can temporarily suspend one's belief in the existence of the external world and produce some kind of ontological equivalence between all intentions whether they are hallucinatory or not, whether they are imaginings, constructs or natural events that are perceived. The view here presented maintains that initially feeling-states are inchoate and undefined and can hypostatically be thought of as occurring without intentionality. They receive their definition through their relation to material events and gain greater precision and specification through the metamorphoses and the re-shuffling of these material events. In this view, consciousness teases its own definition out of the material world. One could call the symbols thus teased out, intentions, if one wishes. But there is no reason why one should look upon such intentionality as the natural condition of mental states without which they cannot occur. To the phenomenologist the act of consciousness is something that is provoked by the object. It is a response to the object.

Phenomenologists say that consciousness is always intentional when, according to the present theory, all they could mean is that consciousness cannot define itself without intending an object. The intentionality necessary for the definition of consciousness or of a state of feeling is, so to speak, a secondary phenomenon. Moreover, there are degrees of intentionality, according to the level of specification of the symbol. A symbol which is a natural event or object is less specified than a symbol which is a metaphor. Therefore, a metaphor is a more specific intention of consciousness than a natural object. But no matter what the degree of specification, once the definition of consciousness has taken place, the intended object (i.e. the designated symbol) is *real*. The reality is defined in terms of the symbol's relation to the state of consciousness and not in terms of relations which natural objects have to one another. Hence a close correspondence between the theory here presented and phenomenology. But the correspondence is not complete. We can define a state of consciousness or of feeling by designating a symbol for it and then 'bracket' the real object intended or suspend a belief in its natural reality.[8] But if the object intended is an image or a dream or a hallucination, there is no need to bracket what is intended, because what is intended has no independent reality but derives *its* reality entirely and exclusively from its relation to the feeling-state. Without the designation of the symbol there would be no definition of the state of consciousness. Where it is difficult to agree with phenomenology is in the contention that a state of consciousness cannot exist or be thought of as an inchoate or undefined state but only as a state that is intentional. According to the present theory, intentionality – to repeat – is a secondary event. But one can agree with phenomenology in the argument that once an intended object is designated as objective correlative, it becomes an integral part of the state of consciousness or of the emotion which would indeed disappear from view without it. For this very reason, however, there is something more arbitrary in the designation of intended objects than phenomenology allows. Again, one can agree that the intended object can be bracketed. It can function as a symbol, that is, whether it is a natural fact, a metaphor or an image of a natural fact, a dream, a hallucination or a memory. In short, its precise ontological status is irrelevant to its functioning as a symbol and the phenomenologist seems right in saying that one can suspend belief in its natural reality – when he means by 'reality' existence in the natural world. The bracketing allows one to equate dreams and real experiences, hallucination and memories, metaphors and images of real experiences. But here again there is a point of difference. In the present theory, the relativity of reality is a fundamental fact. To the phenomenologist, at best, it is an artificially induced belief or a voluntary suspension of judgment so that one can survey the realm of intentions of consciousness freely and without impediment. Hence the doctrine that from the point of view of consciousness all symbols are ontologically equivalent is not so very different from the phenomenological contention that it is possible and desirable from time to time to suspend belief in the external world which would force one to distinguish imaginings from 'real' occurrences. *164714*

The difference between phenomenology and the present view is that in phenomenology the suspension of belief in the natural reality of intended objects is an artificial and temporary exercise. When it is over, we are left with the idea that each act of consciousness intends or reflects a natural event or object; that we love a person because he is lovable and in so far as he is lovable, as Sartre once put it,[9] and so forth. Phenomenology, once its exercise of surveying the intentions of consciousness is concluded, is left with the idea that there is a fixed and unalterable relationship between external facts and states of consciousness which intends those facts. The present theory, on the other hand, considers the relativity of reality as a basic and unalterable condition and hence does not think of the suspension of belief in the external world and the 'bracketing' of intended objects as a temporary and voluntary exercise. The relativity of reality is final and absolute. If one were to speak of suspending belief in the reality of the intended object, one would be indicating that that object is not a symbol assigned to or ascribed to a feeling-state but a naturally intended object without which the feeling-state would not occur. This is hard to accept. In the present view there is first the inchoate feeling-state; then a symbolisation which bestows meaning and definition on the feeling-state. This symbol is real in virtue of its relation to the feeling-state regardless of its ontological status and in spite of the fact that it may well be an artificial construct. The possibility of suspending belief in its reality and of ceasing to suspend that belief and of accepting it as the object intended by the feeling-state – an object which has an independent existence in the external world – does therefore not arise. The suspension of belief is superfluous because there is no need for such a belief in the first place. The reality of the symbol is established by its relation to the feeling-state; not by its relation to other objects in the external world. Our theory need not distinguish between the reality of metaphors and real objects in the external world because it sees the reality of both in terms of their relations to feeling-states.

The theory of the relativity of reality sets the final seal upon our rejection of Lévi-Strauss. Following Hegel, Lévi-Strauss maintains that the primary and primal intellectual experience is the confrontation between subject and perceived object, that is, between self and not-self. Hence the fundamental importance of binary distinctions. Eventually this initial binary categorisation is extended to everything we notice. And thus mythical elaboration is a prolongation of thought itself because it seeks to weave together into one what appear as opposites and binary distinctions: cooked and raw, honey and ashes, male and female, earth and sky, and so forth. As against Hegel, the theory of the relativity of reality does not indentify the first stirring of thought with the experience that the self confronts a not-self; a subject, otherness. It maintains on the contrary that the mind's first awareness of itself stems from the designation of a part or feature of the external world (which includes the human body) as a symbol and then proceeds to more specific awareness by bringing about, through re-shuffling, metaphors and metamorphoses of the external world. Mythical thinking, here, is not so much an extension of thinking about the other, as the very act of thought about thought or mind and its extension to states of greater and more specific self-awareness through an increasing elaboration of metaphor and an increasing transformation of matter. The fact that myths come in typological series and that these series tend towards greater and greater specification then points to the conclusion that mind unfolds itself gradually. From an early condition of unawareness it starts by operating upon the external world, proceeds by transforming it and teasing more and more images out of it until it ends up by formulating an abstract theory about these images, thus reaching a state of abstract self-definition. In this way the mind as it endures through time manages to distinguish its various qualities by making use of the external world. Speaking roughly, these qualities can be summed up as lists of emotions. There is joy and sadness, fear and hope and love and despondency and so forth. But such broad literal descriptions do not do justice to the nuances. And for most states of mind, language has not even a word. Only an elaborate image can pin-point them. Myth, then, is the only way in which the mind can achieve self-definition – not monolithically, but in the sense that its several qualities can rise to awareness and be distinguished from one another.

TWELVE

THE EQUIVALENCE OF SYMBOLS

For many centuries it was believed that the theory of the symbolic equivalence is wrong and that some images, which can have no real status in the natural world, have a status of reality in the supernatural world. This doctrine is not only feeble in view of the arbitrariness with which the images in question are selected; but also feeble in view of the fact that we can have no independent knowledge of the existence of such a duplicate world (supernature) over and above, and independent of, the fact that some images have been selected for privileged status. Since they could have none in the world of nature, the existence of a duplicate world of supernature was postulated. But there was no criterion independent of this postulate for formulating the conditions under which some images had *real* existence in a world other than that of nature. It seems to me that the most persuasive method of overcoming all the difficulties inherent in this doctrine and in the postulate required for its cogency is the theory of the ontological symbolic equivalence of images. This theory refuses to assign different ontological statuses to the various images that function as symbols. It says that as long as images function as symbols, their ontological status is irrelevant. This seems a telling and incontrovertible alternative to the postulate that the natural world ought to be duplicated so that some images can be assigned a status of reality in the duplicate. The theory of symbolic equivalence regardless of ontological status simply obviates the need for such a postulate.

There is powerful and persuasive resistance to the abandonment of this postulate, although of late, owing to the materialistic and secular orientation of western life, it has been less vociferous. But we must face the fact that in one form or another people have always sought to explain the fact that men obey standards of perfection and of goodness which are demonstrably not derived from the observation of this world by postulating that they must have been learnt or observed in another world. The argument has come in many different guises but it always amounts to something like this.[1]

All that we can say is that everything is arranged in this life as though we entered it carrying the burden of obligations contracted in a former life; there is no reason inherent in the conditions of life on this earth that can make us consider ourselves obliged to do good, to be fastidious, to be polite even, nor make the talented artist consider himself obliged to begin over again a score of times a piece of work the admiration aroused by which will matter little to his body devoured by worms, like the patch of yellow wall painted with so much knowledge and skill by an artist who must for ever remain unknown and is barely identified under the name Vermeer. All these obligations which have not their sanction in our present life seem to belong to a different world, founded upon kindness, scrupulosity, self-sacrifice, a world entirely different from this, which we leave in order to be born into this world, before perhaps returning to the other to live once again beneath the sway of those unknown laws which we have obeyed because we bore their precepts in our hearts, knowing not whose hand had traced them there – those laws to which every profound work or the intellect brings us nearer and which are invisible only – and still! – to fools.

In almost all of its forms this argument assumes that our knowledge of these standards of perfection and goodness must be derived from another world. The present argument, however, tends to obviate this recourse to a second world by showing that we can explain the presence of these standards differently. If we assume that these standards are part of the conceptual abstractions of myths, the belief in another world will become superfluous. In this way we can understand why these standards are not part of the ordinary world; and also why, though not part of this ordinary world, they are applicable to it. By reading the typological series backwards, the ordinary world of nature will appear, seen through the slots of the stencil, as consisting of acts where a sheep is not just a helpless victim of human greed but an *agnus Dei*, capable of willing self-sacrifice. The natural world, viewed through the slots of our metaphysical stencils, will thus appear to be 'founded upon kindness, scrupulosity and self-sacrifice, a world entirely different from this world'. But the difference is in appearance only; not in substance. The values and standards of perfection are endemic in the ordinary world of nature. Self-sacrifice happens as much as sacrifice; and beauty as often as ugliness. But without the stencils provided by metaphysics, the endemic values and standards do not appear and remain invisible. Nevertheless, there is only one and the same world. The world in which we see standards of perfection of ethics or aesthetics is not another world, but the one and only world seen from the vantage point of metaphysical abstraction. The quality of human consciousness necessitates the metaphors; the metaphors lead to myths; myths, always under the propulsion of the quality of consciousness, become more and more specific until they converge into metaphysical concepts. And then, if one turns around, one can read the self-same world of nature in the light of these metaphysical concepts, abstracted from the images which the quality of consciousness wrested from nature by re-shuffling and formalisation. But that world of nature will now look very different. Read in the light of these metaphysical concepts, it will appear to have a metaphysical meaning. Giving way to the transposing impetus of the quality of consciousness and proceeding from metaphor to myth and from myth to metaphysics, we will understand the world anew. Where nature was, if we may vary Freud's famous maxim, let metaphysics be. Incidentally, we might add that if we follow this maxim, it might also become slightly easier to realise its psychological model and let *ego* be where *id* was. At any rate, the truth of the matter is that we *do* live in this world burdened by contractual obligations that are not derived from it. But Proust, following a long tradition of Platonism, misinterpreted the situation in thinking that there are two worlds diachronically related. In reality there are only two synchronic appearances of one and the same world.

Unfortunately there is a large school of thought based upon the writings of Bultmann which ignores the theory of symbolic equivalence and seeks to cope with the difficulties admittedly inherent in the postulate of a second, supernatural world by the proposal to *demythologise* those images which have been assigned a status of reality in that duplicate world.[2] The proposal, obviously both necessary and welcome because of the inherent difficulties in the postulate, amounts to no more and no less than a special kind of interpretation of a special mythology. This interpretation is neither structuralist nor functionalist nor typological. But like structuralist and functionalist interpretation of mythology, it is, as its name indicates, a form of demythologisation, a form of deciphering the messages contained in certain myths. It differs from typological interpretation which seeks to allow the myths to reveal themselves through their historical progression towards greater specification. As a form of decoding, it shares in all the disadvantages of structuralism and functionalism without actually partaking in the advantages of either; that is, it even fails to shed light on the sociological importance of the myths in question. Bultmann's decoding is an attempt to translate myths into psychological verities – but it is not universally applicable to all myths and all psychological verities because it concerns itself exclusively with the decoding of Christian mythology and the discovery of the message contained in Heidegger's psychological verities. As long as one seeks to learn something about certain societies and about the manner in which they function, there is, as we have seen earlier, some merit in decoding myths and in seeking to understand the function which the message they contain has in any given society. But when the avowed aim of decoding, as in Bultmann's proposal to demythologise, is to make the myth superfluous by wresting from it a modern psychological verity which the ancients were prevented from expressing in straight language because of their lack of an adequate conceptual framework, no light can be shed on any given society and Bultmann's demythologisation cannot even recommend itself by promising to provide the information which structural and functional analysis and decoding can provide. It stands and falls, therefore, on its ability to cope with the difficulties inherent in the postulate of the duplicate world. But since the theory of the ontological equivalence of symbolic images obviates the need for that postulate, the difficulty with which Bultmann's demythologisation is meant to cope does not really ever arise. Bultmann's method of decoding myth becomes necessary only when the wound is self-inflicted, that is, when one wilfully believes that certain myths about, e.g. the three-deck universe of hell, earth and heaven have an ontological status that is different from the ontological status of a dream or a memory. If the theory of ontological equivalence is accepted, the image of the three-deck universe is an image – no more and no less – and the question as to its precise ontological status is irrelevant as long as it functions as a symbol or objective correlative.

The theory of symbolic equivalence also calls for another comment. The remarks by Collingwood, Cassirer, Oakeshott and Read quoted above draw our attention to the fact that when a symbol is contemplated, be it a natural event or a metaphorical construction, there is an experience of immediacy which removes the distinction between what we normally call real and unreal. I think that when Lévy-Bruhl put forward his theory that primitive people are given to pre-logical thinking, he came, in his psychological terminology, very close to the doctrine of symbolical equivalence. For the quotations from Collingwood, Cassirer, Read and Oakeshott all testify to the immediacy of apprehension of the symbol and they all draw our attention to the fact that what really matters is the method of perception, not the object perceived. The feature which symbols have in common is the immediacy of apprehension, be they natural events or metaphorical constructs. By comparison with that similarity, the possible distinction between those symbols which are 'real' in virtue of their relationship to other parts of the natural world, and the symbols which are 'unreal' or imagined because of their lack of a relationship to parts of the natural world, is minimal and irrelevant. For this reason, I would make a plea, at this late stage, for Lévy-Bruhl. He had put his finger on an important point. Lévi-Strauss's eager overelaboration of his insight that primitive people *are* capable of logical thought, and think in binary distinctions, is likely to cloud the issue. As argued above, there is value and merit in Lévi-Strauss's discovery. But so there is in Lévi-Bruhl's insistence that there is a form of pre-logical thinking. If one strips his insistence of the psychological terminology and replaces the notion of pre-logical thinking with that of immediacy of apprehension, the issue becomes clearer. Lévi-Strauss tried to restore the reputation of primitive people by stressing that, like highly developed rational people, they too can think logically. Lévy-Bruhl, by the same token, can be taken to have vindicated the reputation of primitive people by explaining that they too, like sophisticated poets and mythologists, can apprehend immediately in pure contemplation. The one ability does not exclude the other. On either count, the absolute distinction, which is anathema to Lévi-Strauss, between primitive and non-primitive people, disappears. Both are capable of logic and both are capable of poetry. The real danger with the distinction would be that according to Lévy-Bruhl, poetry was on the side of the primitives, and logic on the side of the moderns. The truth, only partially recovered by Lévi-Strauss, is that both poetry and logic are present in both primitive and modern people.

Lévy-Bruhl had suffered an eclipse long before Lévi-Strauss's critique of the notion of primitive mentality. And even now there is a resistance to reviving the notion because it is so easily linked to the idea of evolution. In fact, it is no exaggeration to say that it plays a vital role in evolutionism and that one cannot think of human evolution except in terms of the notion of primitive as opposed to logical mentality. But the opposite does not hold. Good positivist, liberal evolutionist that Lévy-Bruhl was, he was the worst enemy of his own theory when he called myths strange and incomprehensible tales, absurd narrative which no longer has any effect on us. The demotion of myths to the level of absurdity did not exactly act as a recommendation of primitive mentality. One can and should take Lévy-Bruhl seriously, however, whether one is an evolutionist or not. Even if it is true, as it well might be, that primitive man is capable of logical distinctions between black and white, cooked and raw, dark and light, and classifies everything else accordingly, this does not preclude him from the spontaneous apperception of images. Long ago Vico explained that poetry is not written for aesthetic reasons to delight the mind and adorn a drab world, but that it is a necessity. Imagination, he explained, is not a passive reflection of the external world but the mode in which the mind or spirit becomes aware of itself and assumes a definition by spontaneously shaping the several features of the external world into a concrete image. Imagination thus creates metaphor and myth regardless of the process of logical analysis and the ability to distinguish between A and not-A. 'A whole essay might be written,' said Coleridge, 'on the danger of thinking without images.' But instead of quoting authoritative opinions, it might be more convincing to ponder a description offered by Henry James. Nobody could accuse James of having a primitive mentality. And yet his description of Strether's image of a picture by Lambinet in The Ambassadors is an instance of such a spontaneous perception of a large number of facets of the external world all whirled together into an abiding image which represents a definite state of mind. Strether is travelling in a train through the French countryside and thrilled at the prospect of catching a vision of a landscape as painted by Lambinet. Lambinet's picture, many years ago, had been offered for sale in a Boston gallery. He had not been able to buy it but the memory of the possibility of buying it, the sweetness of this possible adventure, had become suffused in his memory with the sweetness of the landscape in the picture. 'The little Lambinet abode with him ... the particular production that had made him for the moment overstep the modesty of nature.' Henry James comments that 'it would be quite a different thing to see the remembered mixture resolved into its elements – to assist at the restoration of nature of the whole far-away hour: the dusty day in Boston, the background of the Titchburg Depot, of the maroon-coloured sanctum, the special-green vision, the sunny silvery sky, the shady woody horizon.' Here we have a superb description of poetic metaphor, of the mixing of disparate elements (the dusty street in Boston and the sunny silvery sky) which went into the making of the image which abides. Structurally speaking Lévi-Strauss might comment that Strether was able to juxtapose dust with silver. But Henry James tells us that it would be pointless to resolve the image into its elements. The abiding memory of the first vision is *sui generis*. It is a new fact which joins as a complete whole the other facts. It is all important for our understanding of the human mind's workings to keep in front of us the special process of spontaneous mixing of separate elements which makes a complete new element. When Henry James draws our attention to the fact that the various elements, once mixed, cannot be disentangled again he gives a practical demonstration of Suzanne Langer's theory that expressive symbolism (which she distinguishes from practical symbolism like language) forms a whole in the sense that its meaning is not a compound of the discrete elements which constitute it.[3] It would be a pity to remain resistant to this type of awareness because when it is called pre-logical it becomes a necessary postulate in any theory of human evolution. It would be better to drop the term 'pre-logical' and dissociate the phenomenon once and for all from the theory of evolution.

The equivalence of symbolic images, regardless of their ontological status, whether they are natural events or metaphorical constructions, is also borne out by another consideration. It is possible to make a material portrait of any symbol. One can paint it or sculpt it or enact it on the stage of a theatre. If the symbol is a mere natural event, such portrait will amount to no more than a repetition. If the symbolic image is a metaphorical construction, the material representation will be a portrait of the image; but in terms of natural objects, it will be the creation of something new. For when a painter paints a picture or sculptor sculpts a statue or a theatrical producer organises a performance, he is adding a new object or set of objects to the already naturally existing ones. There is no doubt that any symbolic image whatever, no matter how extravagant the metaphor involved, is capable of material representation. This follows directly from our earlier observation that any metaphorical image (and myth is only an extreme instance of such imagery) is due to a re-shuffling of features of events found in nature. And since everything that can be found in nature is capable of material, pictorial representation, so any re-shuffled re-assembly of its various parts is capable of pictorial representation. The resulting picture may look, literally, like nothing on earth. But its several parts will very much look like things on earth.

If every myth is capable of being pictorially represented, it is tempting to class these pictorial products as artifacts. In this case there would be a sharp line of distinction between facts and artifacts. Facts are those events which can be located in nature, somehow in the manner in which, as was suggested above, that facts are auto-chthonous and stand in an automatically emerging relationship to one another. By contrast, artifacts are all those events which are added artificially to naturally existing facts. But little analysis is required to show that this simple distinction cannot hold.[4] To begin with, all artifacts are material objects or events and as such stand in a natural relationship to other natural facts. One can take a photograph of a pictorial presentation of a god and measure the size of the statue of a nymph by relating it to a metric rod. Pictorially presented, therefore, all myths and metaphors become facts in the plain and ordinary sense of the term. Furthermore, there can be no absolute and unequivocal distinction between facts and artifacts. A tree is a fact. A tree sawn into boards is both fact and artifact. And a house built of boards is again both fact and artifact. So is a picture of a man and so is, finally, a picture of a god and the statute of a nymph. In this sense, then, if there is no absolute distinction between facts and artifacts, this lack of distinction underlines the contention that all symbols, be they natural events or metaphorical constructions, are ontologically equivalent. If one tells a story about a tree in order to symbolise a state of mind, one is using a natural fact as symbol. If one embroiders the tree and makes the story into a tale about a tree-god, one is re-shuffling the relationships in which events stand to each other in nature. But if one paints a picture of the tale about the tree-god, one is adding another material and natural object (i.e. the painting) to the already existing object (i.e. the tree). And since one cannot distinguish absolutely between the facticity of the tree and the artifacticity or artificiality of the painting, all the images involved, the tree as well as the tree-god, are symbolically equivalent in ontological status. This is not to deny that from the point of view of practical activity there is always a distinction, albeit not an absolute one, between fact and artifact and, as in the case quoted from *Lord of the Flies*, there is obvious practical value in the ability to draw this distinction. For example: one can live in a real house, but not in a picture of a house. If one cannot make this distinction, one will suffer deadly consequences when one is caught in, say, a snow-storm. For symbolic purposes, there is no need for the distinction; for practical purposes, there is. But even so there is no escaping a certain precariousness in the distinction. For the house is most clearly an artifact like the painting of the house. It is an artifact in a sense in which a cave, which under certain circumstances would do equally well as a shelter in a snow-storm, is not an artifact. Thus even for practical purposes, the distinction between fact and artifact does not run parallel to the distinction between objects with a practical use and objects with a purely aesthetic use.

There is one special case which, on the face of it, does not obviously come under this general theory. It requires special consideration. There is a tale that Jesus Christ was resurrected from the grave. Superficially this tale is very much like countless other tales, all of which contravene the laws of physiology and anatomy and which are therefore to be classed as myths, that is, as tales of events which normally do not happen. But on closer inspection there is a difference between the story about the resurrection and, for example, the story that the goddess Athene sprang from an orifice in the head of Zeus. The story about Jesus and the story about Athene are extreme cases of metaphor. They are composed after separate features and events have been prised loose from the position in which they normally and naturally stand to one another and have been re-assembled in a different way, *sub specie essentiae*. The separate elements, tombs, orifices, births from orifices, revivals and so forth, are all taken from separate parts of the natural world. But in the last analysis, it is claimed that the story about the resurrection happened at a certain time at a certain place, whereas the purveyors of the story about Athene are quite content to preface it by the non-committal remark: 'Once upon a time....' This means that we are invited to take the story about Athene as a simple myth or metaphor, ontologically equivalent to, though *not* equidistant from the state of mind to be symbolised, other stories about births of women or gods. But the story about the resurrection is alleged to be different. Being located at a definite time and place in history rather than introduced by the non-committal statement 'Once upon a time...', the narrator invites his audience to believe that it is more than metaphor; or, if metaphor, that it is a metaphor which actually happened in history; that, in short, it is a miraculous event. The other tales which begin with the formula 'Once upon a time' can hardly be said to be miraculous; for nobody claims that they happened at any particular time in any one particular place. They are, therefore, mere metaphorical images. But if it is claimed that a metaphor actually happened at a particular time, we have nothing less than the claim that a miracle happened.

The question whether miracles happen or do not happen has been debated for centuries. It is widely believed that historical research can throw light on the question of establishing whether in fact, at a specified time and a specified place, the miracle *did* happen. But the historical research that has gone into the matter is pointless. Historians can often prove that certain historical people coined a certain metaphor, i.e., put two separate events together to make one event. But they cannot prove, as historians, that the metaphor is not a metaphor. For history to settle the question whether miracles occur or whether a certain miracle has occurred, it would be necessary to do more than prove historically that somebody coined a certain metaphor. It would also be necessary to prove that a certain metaphor is not a metaphor. But this is precisely what historians for the following reasons cannot do. By and large, to the satisfaction of a great many historians using no canons other than those of ordinary historical investigation, it has been proved that there were indeed some people who, on a certain day in history, found the tomb in question empty and concluded without further ado that Jesus had risen from the dead. The historical evidence for this is perhaps not quite as complete as the evidence for William the Conqueror's victory at Hastings, but the difference is slight. The point is that whatever the difference, it is of no consequence. The people who came to the tomb, found Jesus gone, and concluded that he had risen, were people acting *sub specie essentiae* and therefore construed a metaphor by putting all sorts of events not normally found together into one coherent tale. Suppose someone else had come at the same time to the same tomb but had not been impelled *sub specie essentiae* to construct a metaphor. He would have looked into the tomb and when he found it empty, would have come to the following conclusions. He would have argued that he obviously did not know as much about the physiological state of death as he thought and that people who are dead can return to life. This conclusion would have amounted to his acceptance of the observation of the empty tomb as an empirical falsification of a scientific theory about death and its implications. He would have said that he apparently knew less about death than he thought. It is, however, unlikely that any genuinely scientific observer would have arrived at this conclusion. For a scientifically minded observer would have been more likely to shrug his shoulders about one single, accidental occurrence and, in the absence of repeated observations of the same kind, would have preferred to cling to the established theory of death and its implications and dismiss his particular observation and the empty tomb as a freak. Unwilling to abandon, after one single instance of falsification, his accepted theories of death, he might have concluded, when pressed for an explanation, that either Jesus could not have been really dead when he was put into the tomb or that somebody must have snatched the body or that, perhaps, there had never been an entombment in the first place. And if further historical detective work would have established that Jesus had been buried and had been dead and that the body had *not* been snatched, our scientific observer would still have either taken the observation as a falsification of his theory of what constitutes death, or as a freak to be disregarded. Being disinterested, whichever of these possible conclusions the disinterested observer had come to, none of them would have amounted to a metaphor. No amount of historical research, therefore, can ever throw any light on the matter. For although it is fairly well attested that some people said, on seeing the empty tomb, that Jesus Christ had risen from the dead, there can be no possible 'historical' proof that the metaphorical tale that he had been genuinely dead and had returned to life was a correct version, i.e. something other than a metaphor, and that therefore a miracle had happened. The most telling contribution historical research could make would be to establish that Jesus had been dead and had been buried. But in this case, any disinterested observer of the empty tomb would have been found to say to himself that he obviously did not know as much about the state of death and its disabilities as he thought.

In short, the miraculousness of the event, though an integral part of the tale, cannot itself be proved by historical research. The miraculousness of the event, therefore, is part and parcel of the myth itself. The claim that an event which by all ordinary standards of story-telling is a metaphor or a myth actually took place, as mythically told, in history, must be completely rejected. It follows therefore that, in spite of superficial appearances, the story about the resurrection is basically not different from the story about Athene's birth. It is a clear instance of a myth the raw material of which is not just any natural event like a thunderstorm or the killing of a lamb (events that happen all the time and the significance of which does not depend on their having happened at any particular time at any particular place) but a specific historical event. Historical events, like undated thunderstorms, are natural events. As we have argued earlier, they are often, though not as frequently, taken as the starting point for a typological series of myths. But it makes no difference to a typological series whether the first, unembroidered event which is the raw material, and which is the starting point for a series of typologically progressively embroidered accounts, is a historical event or a commonly occurring natural event. Even thunderstorms and the killing of lambs happen at certain times and certain places. It is conceivable that many a typological series of myths which started with the killing of a lamb took as its point of origin a specific historical slaughter. But for obvious reasons, the specific location in time and place of the slaughter was soon judged irrelevant and then forgotten. Whereas in the present example and some others, it was judged that the historicity of the natural event used as a starting point, was noteworthy and thus continued to be remembered and thus became an integral part of all subsequent stories. But the retention of the historical element makes no substantial difference to the status of the myth. Nor does it add to or detract from the ontological equivalence of all the versions of the story. The natural fact could conceivably have been that people at the time knew less about the state of death than they thought. This fact was then immediately elaborated metaphorically into the myth of resurrection and the historical date was retained as an essential part of the story. The natural, historical fact that Jesus was buried not as dead as people thought, or that what they considered death was not as irrevocable as they thought, was the general, unspecific type. The myth of the resurrection then became the first anti-type. It would not be too difficult to show that, with the help of intervening, progressively specified further anti-types, the final conclusion was reached in the metaphysical doctrine *amor vincit omnia*, Love vanquishes not only Fear but also Death. The last and ultimate, conceptual formulation is highly specific and as such throws a much more revealing light on a certain condition of the human mind than the earliest, natural–historical fact. The various members of the typological chain are therefore not equidistant from the truth to be made manifest; but they are ontologically equivalent.

The truth of the theory of the symbolic equivalence of images depends strictly on the fact that these images function as symbols of states of consciousness. One could also formulate this by saying that the states of consciousness are the only 'reality' there is and that, therefore, the question as to what precisely the ontological status of their objective correlatives are, whether they are natural events or dreams or hallucinations or wishes or hopes or memories of any of these, is completely irrelevant to their ability to function effectively as objective correlatives or symbols.

One of the most fascinating, though completely perverse, modern intellectual experiments ever made is the attempt made by Robbe-Grillet and Butor and their disciples to maintain the ontological equivalence of imagery but to deny at the same time its symbolic function – which is like depriving the theory of the symbolic equivalence of images of its justification *without* denying the truth of the theory.

According to the theory of these writers, the surface of things should cease to be the mask of their heart. These writers treat interiority between brackets – which means in our terminology that they refuse to treat any natural object or event as a potential symbol or objective correlative but insist on treating it merely and exclusively for what it is in itself and for itself. Objects and spaces, as Roland Barthes once put it, and the movements of man from one to the other, are promoted to the rank of subjects. Or, as we might comment, subjects are demoted to the rank of objects.[5] Whichever way one looks at it, the distinction is wiped out. Objects, when treated like this, will gradually lose their uncertainty and their secrets and abandon their false mysteriousness, their dubious interiority which Barthes has christened 'the romantic heart of things'. The 'romantic heart of things' is, however, precisely the emotional state of mind which these objects and events symbolise. If they are deprived of their interiority and their secrets and their mysteriousness (these things are not at all 'false' or 'dubious', except in the sense that they do not naturally form part of the objects and events but attach to them in virtue of their symbolic function or in virtue of their acting as objective correlatives), they must cease to be onto-logically equivalent. If they have no romantic heart, these objects and events are indeed what they are; but in this case they will loudly proclaim whether they are imagined or not, whether they are memo-ries or plans, projections or wishes. In short, deprived of their symbolic efficacy, objects cease to be ontologically equivalent. Some are genuine natural objects; others are revealed as hallucinations or wish-dreams. Robbe-Grillet and Butor and their disciples, however, are not prepared to appreciate this consequence. They want to des-cribe nature and its parts without considering that much of it functions as symbols and at the same time they want to retain the ontological equivalence of all images and refuse to abide by the rational distinction between an imagined stone and a remembered stone and a genuine stone in front of one's eyes. When a kiss between two lovers is a symbol of a state of mind, it becomes irrelevant whether it is a memory of a kiss or a wish for a kiss or a kiss actually taking place. Since the precise ontological status will not affect its symbolic efficacy or prevent it from acting efficiently as an objective correlative, the attempt to define its ontological status is superfluous. But if that same kiss is taken as a surface event which is no longer the mask of its heart, then the interest in its precise ontological status becomes paramount. Robbe-Grillet and Butor cannot have it both ways. Their persistent efforts to have their cake and eat it too have produced one of the most remarkably nonsensical movements in literature. This is not denying its inherent interests. In fact, if one uses their books and films as a raw material and re-invests their sur-faces with the romantic heart their authors seek to deprive them of, one will gain an astonishingly rich system of imagery. For, true to their theory, these writers have indeed treated all their images as ontologically equivalent and have thus succeeded in their films (I am thinking especially of *Last Year in Marienbad*) more than in their books in providing a set of genuinely ontologically equivalent images.[6] Although all images ever used are ontologically equivalent, no other school of writing has been able to present them obviously and manifestly thus with such persistent accuracy of vision because no other school of writing has made the presentation of this equivalence its avowed aim. All one needs to do is to strip Robbe-Grillet's and Butor's works of the perverse contention that the images they contain have no 'dubious interiority' and one will obtain a rich harvest of fascinating imagery. But this imagery needs interpretation, for as the authors present it, it is artificially made to appear as dead and unsymbolic. If it is left thus, it cries out for rational analysis and an assignation of ontological status. Either the stranger in *Last Year in Marienbad* must be interpreted as a symbol of something – in which case it does not matter whether he is a memory, a hallucination, a wish-dream or all of these at different times; or, if he is left uninterpreted as a surface and not a mask of a heart, then one must go to work and find out whether he is in fact a stranger or the man the heroine had met the year before or whether he is a projection of the heroine or her wish-dream.

It would nevertheless be wrong to think of myth, or, for that matter, of all metaphor, as a set of messages about the meaning of those states of feeling or consciousness which are not amenable to literal description. For these feeling-states cannot only not be described literally, they can also not be known or referred to or indicated independently. They receive their meaning or definition or imprint from the metaphor.

> 'And, as imagination bodies forth
> The forms of things unknown, the poet's pen
> Turns them to shapes, and gives to airy nothing
> A local habitation and a name.'
>   (A *Midsummer Night's Dream*, V, i)

Without the metaphor they remain misty and inchoate and one cannot, therefore, look upon the metaphor as a message – unless one is prepared to stretch the meaning of the concept of message sufficiently far. Conventionally, a message draws attention to some condition or state of affairs which exists independently, so that the message is the means of communicating it. In our case, here, however, there is nothing which exists independently and if one looked upon the metaphor as a message one would also have to look upon it at the same time as the phenomenon the message is about. Metaphor and myth, to sum up, do not so much reveal as define the feeling-state. Hence the particular importance that is to be attached to the mythological series which, as it develops typologically and posits ever and ever more specific images, defines the feeling-state more and more precisely.

THIRTEEN

METAPHORS AND SOCIETIES

There is one important difference between our need for ordinary
metaphor and the re-shuffled images that present themselves in myths
and dreams, tales and legends. Ordinary metaphor is a strictly
linguistic phenomenon and as such rarely transcends any particular
language or language group. It is also culture-conditioned in the
sense that in any one language, metaphorical conventions can come
and go. But the cultivation and communication of myth transcends
linguistic barriers and stretches over vast regions of time and
comprehends the most diverse peoples. Some societies or churches,
from time to time, take it upon themselves to cultivate a particular
set of myths and preserve and hand it down in a certain particular
form and degree of specification. But such temporary orthodoxies
are accidental. They are due to the fact that some societies make use
of myth for purposes of social bonding or coherence. They have no
more and no less to do with the longevity of myth than the fact that
the harnessing of water in a mill influences its power and flow from
the tops of distant mountains to the oceans. The social use of
mythology is fortuitous and accidental. It is a great pity that most
scholars are too cautious to let go of the social setting in which they
find the source material for any particular myth or any particular
shape of any particular myth. They feel compelled to keep their feet
on the ground and relate the myth to the setting through the agency
of which they have obtained knowledge of its existence. The importance of the method by which we know of myths cannot be denied.
Myths are important social and cultural facts because the sharing of
myths is an essential aspect of their existence. But their sociological
anchorage must not be allowed to cloud the issue. The point is worth
stressing. As a result of the development of sociology we have all
become very accustomed to the idea that myth and ritual and indeed

118

all religion serves an important function in keeping society together. We have therefore come to understand the anchorage of myth and ritual in society in one sense and one sense only. We always inquire what religion does for society and forget that the mere fact of anchorage must just as readily lead to the opposite question: what does society do for religion in general and for myth and ritual in particular? Durkheim and his innumerable followers are, of course, the protagonists of the first inquiry. Many theologians have come close to asking the second question but it always looks as if they do not quite dare to consider society in general or any one social order in particular as the handmaid to the truth they are seeking. They feel hesitant because if they pursued the question it would look as if they were blowing their own trumpet. Arnold Toynbee's philosophy of history comes closest to looking at the relation between society and religion in an anti-Durkheim light. Toynbee argues that civilisations or societies give birth to religions which transcend them. He sees societies as the occasions for an epiphany of a higher religion and looks upon those societies as the chrysalis of metaphysical truth. Here we have an acceptance of the anchorage but an inquiry based not on the question how religion helps to keep society together but on the question what service a social order can render to religion. Any sociological approach – and since myth cannot float in mid-air there must be a sociological approach – has to face both ways. When one is interested in society, one starts with Durkheim. When one is interested in the self-revelation of the human mind, one must follow Toynbee. For our present argument we should not consider the role of religion in society but the role of society in religion. If the preceding argument is accepted, one should see that the history of mythical tales, their unilinear development towards greater and greater specification until it reaches the point of conceptual metaphysical doctrine, should be treated as the self-revelation of the human mind. This latter thesis is to be taken in a concrete sense. In so far as myth defines the states of consciousness not amenable to literal description, the ultimately specified form of a myth is the ultimate revelation of the quality of the state of consciousness of which it is the non-literal, symbolic, expression. Any society, therefore, of which the myth is a social institution mediates between nature and truth. For initially, the myth is a slight transformation of natural events into a mythical tale; and in the end, highly specific, the mythical tale is a quasi-conceptual formulation of the precise quality of states of feeling. Unfortunately, most modern observers and students of mythology mistake the communication of myth in societies for the reason for its existence. But the cultivation of myth by a society as part of its social institutions is only the temporary form of its existence, not the reason for its existence. If the form of existence of myth is mistaken for its *raison d'être*, it appears only too easily as a message. And then the conclusion that that message is either a charter for social action (Malinowski) or a conciliation of conflicts (Lévi-Strauss) is all too readily at hand. It appears to me that societies, by being the carriers of myth for whatever socially useful or practical purpose (such as legitimising certain institutions or providing an anchorage for the present in the past or for expressing social solidarity), are the mediators between the metaphysical truths we have come to know, and the natural events which make these truths plausible. But mediation, no matter what its social purpose, should not be equated with the reason for the existence of myth.

We should end with an invocation of Vico. Like so many other thinkers of a later, more romantic age, Vico spotted that the typological series owes its beginning, its bottom layer, to a child-like spontaneous sense of imagery and proceeds gradually towards rational reflection on that imagery. Though capable of serving as the basis for a theory of evolution, in Vico's hands this view remained comparatively neutral. For unlike Lévy-Bruhl and all other modern evolutionists, Vico was innocent of the idea that mankind is divided into many different and separate societies or civilisations which stand to each other in an evolutionary relationship. It was not part of his scheme to think that some societies present an early or primitive state of development and others a late and intellectually sophisticated stage. He looked at mankind as an indivisible whole. For good or for ill his view of the importance and role of child-like sensation applied to the earliest time of mankind as a whole. No doubt, he took this to have a serious historical application. But we could reinterpret him and think of it in a less historico-evolutionary manner, especially since we would not think of evolution, if we do at all, as something that had affected mankind as a unitary whole. We are therefore free to take it that he saw myth, which was the first and most significant single creation of child-like sensation and immediacy of unreflective perception of metaphor ('The first utterances,' Rousseau said, 'were tropes', to be echoed by Goethe: 'One thinks one is talking pure prose and is really speaking in tropes'), as something that needs a society for its origin and cultivation but also as something that transcends any one society. Once started, the series would sooner or later reach its top, regardless of any society. Hence his magnificent sweep of understanding. The ultimate metaphysical truths, he realised, emerge as the top of the series. They are timeless in their truth and application but are reached at the end of long chains of typologically ordered images. Societies are the carriers of the myths which mediate between truth and nature. The truth itself, the Idea, is beyond time; but the mediating evidence is not. In Platonic thought and in every philosophy that was derived from it, there had been an unbridgeable gulf between time and Idea, the particular and the universal, becoming and being. The gulf remained unbridgeable even when modern evolutionist thinking reversed Plato's evaluation of it. Plato had believed that truth was on the side of Idea and that becoming was a form of illusion. Modern evolutionism stood Plato on his head; but the dichotomy remained. Vico's explanation eliminated the gulf. The Truth of Idea depended on the temporal extension of the typological series. The truth about mind – and it was only with mind that he was concerned – unfolds with the passing of time and if it were not for the passing of time, the series could not develop towards its abstract top, the Idea. In this sense, the present participates in the past, because the Idea's truth is distilled as a result of the temporal extension of the typological series of images; and the past participates in the present, because the Idea emerges as a result of the ever-increasing specificity of the imagery. The process is unilineal and irreversible. But the metaphysical truth which is its end-product can cause an incessant feed-back so that the rawest perception of nature can be made to appear as a *praeparatio evangelica*.

NOTES

Chapter Two   A Critique of Structuralism

1 See E. H. Gombrich, *Art and Illusion*, London, 1962 ed., pp. 273-4.
   Unfortunately he says nothing about the Picasso variations of the theme.
2 *Structuralism*, New York, 1970, p. 113.
3 And yet, it should be pointed out at this early stage, that Lévi-Strauss's use
   creates its own limitations. Consider Manet's picture *Le Déjeuner sur
   l'herbe* both in relation to Raimondi's etching and to Picasso's variations.
   A structuralist view of the series will disclose nothing beyond the discovery
   that there is a relation both between the nude in Manet's painting and her
   formal predecessor in Raimondi's etching and her successor, if it can still
   be called a nude, in any of Picasso's variations, on one side; and, on the
   other side, that there is a relation between the nude in Manet's painting
   and her companion's walking stick; and the nude and the reed of flax in
   Raimondi's etching. Structurally, the several elements in the series can be
   sorted out both vertically and horizontally and that is all. In fact, a
   consideration of the temporal relationship between the works of Raimondi,
   Manet and Picasso will reveal much more than that. If one takes Raimondi's
   etching as the *typos* and the others as anti-types, one will stumble upon the
   growing specification involved in the series. One will be led from Raimondi's
   nude figures to Manet's naked woman and her dressed companions
   towards Picasso's complete abstractions. The order thus revealed will not
   be due to the process employed in sorting out the separate elements either
   horizontally and vertically and the consequent discovery that there are
   relationships which hold vertically and others which hold horizontally.
   Considered typologically, the series reveals, as Proust defined it with an
   ironic pun on Manet's title, 'the cruel law of art ... that people die and
   that we ourselves die ... so that the grass, not of oblivion but of eternal
   life, grass rich of fertile works may grow ... so that thither, gaily and
   without a thought for those who are sleeping beneath them, future
   generations may come to enjoy their *déjeuner sur l'herbe*'. (*Le Temps
   retrouvé*, II, Paris, 1927, pp. 247-8; author's translation.)
4 W. H. Auden, *Making, Knowing and Judging*, Oxford, 1956, p. 19.
5 Quoted by F. Kermode, 'The Words and the World', *Encounter*, 14, 4, 1960,
   p. 47. The same point is now made by N. Chomsky, *Problems of Knowledge
   and Freedom*, Fontana, 1972, p. 24: 'meaning need not involve communication'.

Chapter Four The Phenomenon of Typology

1 'The Structural Study of Myth', in T. A. Sebeok, ed., *Myth*, Bloomington, 1958, p. 57.

2 The truth of the matter is that there is *no* theme-and-variations; for the various variations are all we have. At the most, the theme is a summary. It is remarkable that with his insistence that there is a theme and so many variations and that the variations, if necessary, ought to be 'corrected' in the light of the theme, Lévi-Strauss comes close to adopting Jung's Platonic theory that myths are archetypes and that each version is nothing but a particular instance of the general. Unlike Jung, Lévi-Strauss draws no further conclusions from this. But the similarity is noteworthy.

3 G. S. Kirk, *Myth*, Cambridge, 1970, pp. 50 and 74.

4 Percy S. Cohen, *Man*, n.s., 4, 1969, p. 351.

5 Alister Cameron, *The Identity of Oedipus the King*, New York, 1968.

6 J. Fontenrose, *Python, A Study of the Delphic Myth and its Origins*, Berkeley, 1959.

7 The lesson is spelt out in E. H. Erikson, *Childhood and Society*, Pelican, p. 272.

8 I have drawn on the following works: S. N. Kramer, *Sumerian Mythology*, Philadelphia, 1944; S. H. Hooke, *Middle Eastern Mythology*, Harmondsworth (Pelican Books), 1963; S. G. F. Brandon, *Creation Legends of the Ancient Near East*, London, 1963; W. K. C. Guthrie, *In the Beginning*, London, 1957; H. Gunkel, *Schöpfung und Chaos in Urzeit und Endzeit*, Göttingen, 1921.

The creation story of the Old Testament is an anti-type of the Babylonian creation myth. The story of the seduction of Adam into evil and the loss of innocence has an earlier type in the Epic of Gilgamesh. The Epic itself goes back to Sumerian, pre-Babylonian times. Cf. S. Kramer, *History Begins at Sumer*, Anchor Books, 1959, pp. 182–99. But whatever pre-Biblical version we take, the story is more general, more naturalistic, less morally explicit than the Biblical version. Enkidu, the Mesopotamian Adam, met a harlot. She 'uncovered her breast and spread her legs, and he possessed her luxuriousness. She felt no shyness, but took his penis, loosened her clothes, and he lay on her. She did a woman's work and made him lascivious and he mounted on her back.' (S. A. Pallis, *The Antiquity of Iraq*, Kopenhagen, 1956, p. 681.) The Biblical anti-type (Genesis I, 2, xv–I, 3, xxiv) is morally more explicit about the implications of Adam's loss of innocence and more symbolic about the precise part played by Eve and the phallic serpent. The earlier Mesopotamian version could mean almost anything. The later Biblical anti-type, though still open to many varying and conflicting interpretations, provides some guide-lines as to meaning by linking the loss of innocence to a moral decision. For more examples see A. Heidel, *The Gilgamesh Epic and Old Testament Parallels*, Chicago, 1946. Heidel, like so many other scholars, is very aware of the parallels but shows little sensitivity to the fact that the later versions are anti-types, i.e., more specific and more elaborate in their symbolism. Consider for example the special role of the serpent. In the Gilgamesh Epic, the serpent steals the flower of immortality which Gilgamesh has laboriously retrieved from the depth of the sea. (Cf. S. N. Kramer, *op. cit.*, p. 187, and G. Bibby, *Looking for Dilmun*, Penguin Books, 1972, p. 173, and A. Heidel, *op. cit.*, p. 10.) The serpent by nothing more than an act of natural greed deprives man of immortality. In the Biblical versions the serpent assumes a phallic role, becomes specifically an adversary of God and the effect of its malevolent interference in the cosmic economy is something much more subtly complex than the mere loss of immortality.

9 H. G. Güterbock, 'The Hittite version of the Hurrian Kumarbi myths: oriental forerunners of Hesiod', *American Journal of Archeology*, 52, 1948; P. Walcot, 'The texts of Hesiod's Theogony and the Hittite Epic of Kumarbi', *Classical Quarterly*, 6, 1956. Cf. M. L. West, *Hesiod's Theogony*, Oxford, 1966, pp. 20–2, 27, 28–30; and P. Walcot, *Hesiod and the Near East*, Cardiff. 1966, pp. 1–26 and especially p. 33 on the dates of Hesiod's *Theogony*, the Hittite Epic and the Babylonian Epic. Walcot points out that the Hattusas tablets are most probably earlier (circa 1400–1200 B.C.) than the now accepted date of *Enuma Elish* (circa 1100 B.C.). One can therefore not look upon the Hittite Epic as a missing link in the typological series. It is most probably not an anti-type of *Enuma Elish*. It is more likely an anti-type of earlier versions of the Babylonian Epic and, in turn, together with the Babylonian Epic one of the types of the *Theogony*.

10 F. M. Cornford, *Principium Sapientiae*, Cambridge, 1952.

11 For metaphysical abstraction from mythical imagery in Hebrew thought and Christian philosophy see the works of Gilson and Tresmontant below in Bibliographical Appendix, 5.

12 Cornford explored a typological series on a vast scale. On a smaller scale, to give an example, typology is equally present in the emergence of the ancient Egyptian Memphite theology. There was no carry over into either Greece or the Old Testament and therefore, for obvious reasons, this typological series was never carried forward to spectacular results in metaphysical doctrine. The Memphite theology is an anti-type of the older story in which Atum comes into being out of Nūn. The newer Memphite theology does not discard the older story but specifies it by identifying Nūn (primeval waters) as Ptah (heart and tongue). See J. A. Wilson, 'Egypt' in: H. and H. A. Frankfort, eds, Bibliographical Appendix, 6, pp. 65–70; S. G. F. Brandon, *op. cit.*, pp. 30ff.; R. T. Rundle Clark, *Myth and Symbol in Ancient Egypt*, London, 1959, pp. 60–7; S. Morenz *Ägyptische Religion*, Stuttgart, 1960, pp. 181ff; H. Frankfort, *Ancient Egyptian Religion*, New York, 1948, pp. 20–1. It is perhaps indicative that G. S. Kirk, *op. cit.*, p. 208, although he quotes both Wilson and Rundle Clark, can see nothing but 'random' and 'inconsistent' development in Egyptian mythology. According to older authorities, the Aten cult was a revolutionary departure from ancient mythology. Cyril Aldred, *Akhenaten*, London, 1972, p. 162 (Abacus ed.), takes pains to point out that the Aten was really a typological specification of the ancient falcon-headed man bearing the sun-disk on his head. He was now represented 'by an abstract symbol, the elaborated glyph for sunlight, a disk encircled by a uraeus with an *ankh* life-sign depending from its neck and having a dozen or more rays ending in his hands'.

Chapter Five   The Opportunism of Structuralism

1 E. Leach in *Discovery*, 23, 1962.

2 For this analysis I have availed myself of the commentaries on Hesiod by M. L. West, *Hesiod's Theogony*, Oxford, 1966 and S. G. F. Brandon, *Creation Legends of the Ancient Near East*, London, 1963, pp. 166ff.

3 M. Proust, *Time Regained*, English trans., London, 1944, pp. 411–14.
4 As against a structuralist approach, cf. O. I. Holtan, *Mythic Patterns in Ibsen's Last Plays*, Minneapolis, 1970.

Chapter Six Typological Interpretation

1 Cp. the celebrated book by R. Otto, *The Holy*, English trans., London, 1923.
2 H. and H. A. Frankfort *et al.*, *Before Philosophy*, Harmondsworth (Pelican Books), 1949; first published as *The Intellectual Adventure of Ancient Man*, Chicago, 1946.
3 Michael Grant, *Roman Myths*, London, 1971, p. 222. See G. Dumézil, *Servius et la Fortune*, Paris, 1943, pp. 189–93, and the same author's *Jupiter, Mars, Quirinus*, Paris, 1941, and *Horace et les Curiaces*, Paris, 1942, and now in English translation, 'Myth and Epic', in *The Destiny of the Warrior*, Chicago and London, 1970.
4 I have used material from the works of H. Zimmer and A. Coomaraswamy, see below, Bibliographical Appendix, 5; as well as the following: M. Eliade, *Yoga; Immortality and Freedom*, English trans., London, 1958; S. Radhakrishnan, *The Brāhma Sutra*, London, 1960; H. Oldenberg, *Die Religion des Veda*, Stuttgart, 1917.

Chapter Seven Myths and Metaphysics

1 The possibility of re-projection depends on the phenomenon of typology. There can be no meaningful re-projection unless there is a typological series. Re-projection is at the heart of Pico's Cabalistic magic: 'magicam operari non est aliud quam maritare mundum' (cf. F. A. Yates, *Giordano Bruno and the Hermetic Tradition*, London, 1964, p. 88). More ancient and more time-honoured is the principle of Vedic method: 'yo evam veda' cf. H. Zimmer, *Kunstform und Yoga*, Berlin, 1926, p. 177; and H. Oldenberg, *Die Lehre der Upanishaden*, Göttingen, 1923, p. 22.). The sexual union of man and woman is the type of the return of multiplicity into the undifferentiated One. He who knows that ('yo evam veda') there is such a typological relationship between a natural act and a metaphysical doctrine, Zimmer explains, will be able to understand the former in the light of the latter. For this reason A. Coomaraswamy, see below, Bibliographical Appendix, 5, argued that there is a complete parallelism between the doctrine of the Self and the doctrine of God — autology = theology. See also H. Oldenberg, *op. cit.*, p. 21; and Agehananda Bharati, *The Tantric Tradition*, London, 1965, pp. 19–20. I cannot understand why Agehananda Bharati thinks that Sankara's employment of the ancient principle 'yo evam veda' must be due to Tantric influence. I am not invoking Vedic thought or the Hermetic Tradition, Cabala or Neoplatonism or the famous theory of the fourfold meaning of Scripture, all of which presuppose typological relationships, as a justification for re-projection. On the contrary, I am quoting these examples of re-projection in order to show that the typology on which they depend has always been widely recognised. For typology in the Cabala see G. Scholem, *Zur Kabbala und ihrer Symbolik*, Zürich, 1960, p. 177; in Muslim mysticism, F. Meier, 'Der Derwischtanz', *Asiatische Studien*, 7, 1954, pp. 118–19; in alchemy, C. G. Jung, 'Erlösungsvorstellungen in der Alchemie', *Eranos Jahrbuch*, Zürich, 1936.

2 Cited after Mary Douglas, 'The Meaning of Myth', in E. Leach, ed., *The Structural Study of Myth and Totemism*, London, 1967, p. 51.

3 To date, unfortunately, only four of the projected volumes have appeared : C. H. Long, *Alpha, The Myths of Creation*; J. L. Henderson and Maud Oakes, *The Wisdom of the Serpent, The Myths of Death, Rebirth and Resurrection*; A. W. Watts, *The Two Hands of God, The Myths of Polarity*; and J. W. Perry, *Lord of the Four Quarters*; all published by George Braziller, New York, 1963– .

4 Rudolf Carnap, *Philosophy and Logical Syntax*, English trans., London, 1935, p. 28.

5 Cp. for instance G. Ryle, *Plato's Progress*, Cambridge, 1966. I. M. Crombie, *An Examination of Plato's Doctrines*, London, 1962, Vol. 1, p. 153, says that the purpose of some myths is that the reader may 'by the process of "drawing the moral" learn the region within which in Plato's view the truth is to be found'. This is a little equivocal but could be taken to mean something approaching the present argument. W. Bröcker, *Plato's Gespräche*, Frankfurt, 2nd ed., 1967, p. 211, takes a view explicitly opposed to my argument when he says that Plato first lays the rational foundation which the myth presupposes. Of all recent scholars P. Friedländer, *Plato*, English trans., New York, 1958, Vol. 1, pp. 193, 209, without committing himself to an explicit view, is the most sensitively appreciative of the mythical presuppositions of Plato's abstract doctrines. For further discussion see P. Munz, *Relationship and Solitude*, London, 1964, pp. 86–8. The closest support for the argument that Plato's metaphysics is abstracted from the myths comes from J. A. Stewart, *The Myths of Plato*, G. Levy, ed., London, 1961.

6 It seems strange that this connection went unnoticed by E. W. Knight, *Literature Considered as Philosophy*, London, 1957.

Chapter Eight   Metaphysics and Symbols

1 Herbert Read, *English Prose Style*, New York, 1952, p. 23.

2 P. Wheelwright, *Metaphor and Reality*, Bloomington, 1962, p. 71; W. K. Wimsatt, *The Verbal Icon*, University of Kentucky Press, 1954, p. 79.

3 This argument is an extrapolation from F. A. Hayek's *The Sensory Order*, London, 1952. Hayek tried to show that we never perceive unique properties of individual objects; but always properties which the objects have in common with other objects. Perception is, therefore, always an interpretation and classification. The present argument extrapolates that a large proportion of our daily perceptions are metaphorical images rather than perceptions of individual facts.

4 *Essai sur l'origine des langues*, London, 1783, p. 565: 'The first utterances were tropes.'

5 *Biology and Knowledge*, Edinburgh, 1971.

6 See T. S. Eliot, in Bibliographical Appendix, 8, below. Mallarmé, *Oeuvres Complètes*, p. 869, had made the same point. He described the creation of a symbol as the art of choosing an object and extracting from it an 'état d'âme'. Mallarmé's statement is the *locus classicus*.

7 J. N. Findlay, *Gifford Lectures – The Discipline of the Cave* and *The Transcendance of the Cave*, London, 1966 and 1967.

8 This theory of the emergence of abstract art differs substantially from the theories developed by Worringer, Gilson and Ehrenzweig. It is incompatible

with Worringer's, but not necessarily with Gilson's and Ehrenzweig's. It will help to explain many points raised by Wind and by Rosenberg. For all these works see below, Bibliographical Appendix, 10. H. Wölfflin, *Principles of Art History*, 1st German ed. 1915, English trans. 1932 of 7th German ed., has attempted to turn this inner momentum of every school into a developmental philosophy of the history of art.

9 The description of algolagnia is by E. Dühren, *Der Marquis de Sade und seine Zeit*, Berlin, 1901, pp. 414–15.

Chapter Nine Symbols and Signs

1 Guy E. Swanson, *Religion and Regime*, Ann Arbor, 1967.
2 E. Topitsch, *Vom Ursprung und Ende der Metaphysik*, Vienna, 1958.
3 H. Werner, *Die Ursprünge der Metaphor*, Leipzig, 1919.
4 C. Kluckhohn, 'Myths and Rituals', *Harvard Theological Review*, 35, 1942.
5 R. Barthes, *Critique et vérité*, Paris, 1966; R. Picard, *Nouvelle critique ou nouvelle imposture?*, Paris, 1965; cf. J. Josipovici, *The World and the Book*, London, 1971, pp. 268–85.

Chapter Ten Symbols and Psychology

1 H. F. Searle, 'The Effort to Drive the Other Person Crazy', *British Journal of Medical Psychology*, 32, 1959.
2 R. D. Laing, *The Divided Self*, London, 1960, *passim*.
3 S. Freud, *Studies on Hysteria*, standard ed., Vol. 2, p. 263.
4 Harry Guntrip, *Personality Structure and Human Interaction*, London, 1961, p. 155.
5 Paul Ricoeur, *Freud and Philosophy*, New Haven, 1970, Book 1.

Chapter Eleven The Truth Value of Symbols

1 Cp. E. E. Evans-Pritchard, *Nuer Religion*, Oxford, 1956, p. 128, and E. Gellner, Bibliographical Appendix, 1.
2 R. G. Collingwood, *The Principles of Art*, paperback ed., Oxford, 1963, p. 136.
3 E. Cassirer, *The Philosophy of Symbolic Forms*, New Haven, 1955, Vol. 2, p. 261.
4 Herbert Read, *The Forms of Things Unknown*, London, 1960, pp. 113–14.
5 M. Oakeshott, *Rationalism in Politics and Other Essays*, London, 1962, p. 217.
6 Ronald Fairbairn, *Psychoanalytic Studies of the Personality*, London, 1953, p. 9.
7 See p. 57f, above.
8 The technical term used by Husserl for this suspension is *epoché* – an act of withdrawal from the usual assertive consciousness regarding what does and does not exist in the world.
9 Quoted by J. F. Revel, *On Proust*, English trans., London, 1972, p. 34. Revel comments pointedly that life inflicts innumerable proofs to the contrary. One might add that love is rarely in proportion to the lovability of the person loved. It is usually less and sometimes more. This may be a cause for regret but there is perhaps consolation in the thought that if we all got what we deserved, things would be even worse. The impossibility of

assessing objectively the due degree of love one should have for a person or the commensurate amount of fear is a telling proof of the truth of the doctrine of the relativity of reality and of the dependence of the reality of symbols upon the feeling-states they define and bestow meaning on rather than on their relation to objects in the external world.

Chapter Twelve   The Equivalence of Symbols

1   M. Proust, *Remembrance of Things Past*, English trans. by C. K. Scott Moncrieff, London, 1949, IX, pp. 250–1.
2   Apart from the well-known works of Bultmann, see J. Macquarrie and L. Malevez in Bibliographical Appendix, 6, below.
3   *Philosophy in a New Key*, Cambridge Mass., 3rd ed., 1963, p. 96.
4   J. Monod begins the first chapter of *Chance and Necessity*, London, 1972, by pointing out that there is neither a simple nor an absolute distinction between fact and artifact.
5   'Une littérature objective', *Critique*, July, 1954; cf. also J. Sturrock, *The French Novel*, London, 1968; J. G. Weightman, 'Robbe-Grillet', *Encounter*, 102, 1962.
6   See P. Munz, 'Five Evenings in Marienbad', *Landfall*, 67, 1963.

BIBLIOGRAPHICAL APPENDIX

The following, highly selective, lists are not so much a bibliography of the many subjects discussed in this book as a substitute for lengthy references to important works in notes; their inclusion has made it possible to keep the notes to a minimum. Entries with an asterisk contain bibliographies. Obvious classics such as Frazer and Freud, Durkheim and Toynbee, Coleridge and Goethe are omitted.

1. The Theory of Myth (see chapters 1 and 13)

ALTIZER, T. J. J., et al., eds, Truth, Myth and Symbol, Engelwood Cliffs, New Jersey, 1962.
BUESS, E., Geschichte des mythologischen Erkennens, München, 1953.
CAMPBELL, J., The Flight of the Wild Gander, New York, 1969.
COHEN, P.S., 'Theories of Myth', Man, n.s., 4, 1969.
ELIADE, M., Myth and Reality, English trans., New York, 1959.
ELIADE, M., The Sacred and the Profane, New York, 1959.
FUHRMANN, M., ed., Terror und Spiel, Probleme der Mythenrezeption, München, 1971.
GELLNER, E., 'Concepts and Society', in B. R. Wilson, ed., Rationality, Oxford, 1970.
HÖNIGSWALD, R., Vom erkenntnistheoretischen Gehalt alter Schöpfungserzählungen, Stuttgart, 1957.
HORTON, R., 'African Traditional Thought and Western Science', in B. R. Wilson, ed., Rationality, Oxford, 1970.
JACKSON, W. F., Cumaean Gates, Oxford, 1936.
JACOBI, J., Complex, Archetype, Symbol, in the Psychology of C. G. Jung, London, 1959.
KERENYI K., ed., Die Eröffnung des Zugangs zum Mythos, Darmstadt, 1967.
KIRK, G. S., Myth, Cambridge, 1970.
KITAGAMA, J. M., et al., eds., Myths and Symbols, Chicago, 1969.
LEACH, E., 'Frazer and Malinowski', Encounter, 146, 1965.
LÉVY-BRUHL, L., Primitive Mentality, English trans., London, 1923.
MALINOWSKI, B., Myth in Primitive Psychology, London, 1926.
*PÉPIN, J., Mythe et Allégorie, Paris, 1958.
PETTAZZONI, R., 'Die Wahrheit des Mythos', Paideuma, 4, 1950.
RADCLIFFE-BROWN, A. R., 'Religion and Society', in A. R. Radcliffe-Brown, Structure and Function in Primitive Society, London, 1952.
ROBINSON, T. H., 'Hebrew Myths', in S. H. Hooke, ed., Myth and Ritual, Oxford, 1933.

K

SEBEOK, TH. A., ed., *Myth*, Bloomington, 1958.
SLOCHOVER, H., *Mythopoesis*, Detroit, 1970.
SLOTE, B., ed., *Myth and Symbol*, Lincoln, 1963.
*VICKERY, J. B., ed., *Myth and Literature*, Lincoln, 1966.
VOLKMANN-SCHLUCK, K. H., *Mythos und Logos; Interpretation en zu Schellings Philosophie der Mythologie*, Berlin, 1969.
VRIES, J. DE, *Forschungsgeschichte der Mythologie*, München, 1961.

2. Histories of Mythological Motifs (see chapter 4)

BOWRA, M., *A Heritage of Symbolism*, London, 1943.
BRIFFAULT, R., *The Mothers*, English trans., London, 1952.
BUSH, D., *Mythology and the Renaissance Tradition in English Poetry*, Minneapolis, 1932.
BUSH, D., *Mythology and the Romantic Tradition in English Poetry*, Cambridge, Mass., 1937.
BUTLER, E. M., *The Myth of the Magus*, Cambridge, 1948.
BUTTERWORTH, E. A. S., *The Tree at the Navel of the Earth*, Berlin, 1970.
*CAMERON, A., *The Identity of Oedipus the King*, New York, 1968.
CAMPBELL, J., *The Hero with the Thousand Faces*, New York, 1961.
COMPARETTI, D., *Virgilio nel medioevo*, Firenze, 1896.
EISLER, R., *Weltenmantel und Himmelszelt*, München, 1910.
ELIADE, M., *Pattern in Comparative Religion*, English trans., London, 1960.
FONTENROSE, J., *Python*, Berkeley, 1959.
FORTES, M., *Oedipus and Job in West African Religion*, Cambridge, 1959.
*GALINSKY, G. K., *The Heracles Theme*, Oxford, 1972.
GASTER, T. H., *Myth, Legend and Custom in the Old Testament*, London, 1969.
GRAVES, R., *The White Goddess*, London, 1961.
HOCART, A. M., *The Life-Giving Myth*, London, 1952.
HOLMBERG, V., *Der Baum des Lebens*, Helsingfors, 1922.
*JAMES, E. O., *The Cult of the Mother Goddess*, London, 1959.
JUNG, G. and KERENYI, K., *Introduction to a Science of Mythology*, London, 1951.
KLINZ, A., *Hieros Gamos*, Halle, 1933.
MACKENZIE, D. A., *The Migration of Symbols*, London, 1926.
NEUMANN, E., *The Great Mother*, New York, 1955.
*PESTALOZZA, U., *Eterno Feminino Mediterraneo*, Venice, 1954.
PETTAZZONI, R., *The All-Knowing God*, English trans., London, 1956.
PICARD, C., *Die grosse Mutter von Kreta bis Eleusis*, Zürich, 1938.
PRZYLUSKI, J., *La Grande Déesse*, Paris, 1950.
ROBERTSON, S., *Rosegarden and Labyrinth*, London, 1963.
SEZNEC, J., *The Survival of the Pagan Gods*, English trans., London, 1953.
SLOCHOVER, H., *Mythopoesis*, Detroit, 1970.
STANFORD, W. B., *The Ulysses Theme*, Oxford, 1963.
STRAUSS, W. A., *Descent and Return: The Orphic Theme in Modern Literature*, Cambridge, Mass., 1971.
STRICH, F., *Die Mythologie in der deutschen Dichtung von Klopstock bis Wagner*, Berlin, 1910.
SUHR, E. G., *The Mask, The Unicorn and The Messiah; a Study in Solar Eclipse Symbolism*, New York, 1970.
VANGAARD, T., *Phallos*, Kopenhagen, 1969.
VINGE, L., *The Narcissus Theme in Western European Literature*, Lund, 1967.
WATTS, A. W., *Myth & Ritual in Christianity*, London, 1954.

WEINSTEIN, L., *The Metamorphoses of Don Juan*, New York, 1967.
WHEELWRIGHT, P. E., *The Burning Fountain*, Bloomington, 1968.
WITT, R. E., *Isis in the Graeco-Roman World*, London, 1971.

3. Structuralism (see chapter 2)

BOON, J. A., *From Symbolism to Structuralism*, Oxford, 1972.
*BOUDON, R., *The Uses of Structuralism*, London, 1971.
*LANE, M., ed., *Structuralism*, London, 1970.
*LEACH, E., ed., *The Structural Study of Myth and Totemism*, London, 1967.
LEACH, E., *Lévi-Strauss*, London, 1970.
LÉVI-STRAUSS, C., 'The Structural Study of Myth', *Journal of American Folklore*, 68, 1955, and in T. A. Sebeok, ed., *Myth*, Bloomington, 1958.
LEPENIES, W., ed., *Orte des wilden Denkens*, Frankfurt, 1970.
LÉVI-STRAUSS, C., *La Pensée sauvage*, Paris, 1962.
LÉVI-STRAUSS, C., *Le Cru et le Cuit*, Paris, 1964.
LÉVI-STRAUSS, C., *Du Miel aux Cendres*, Paris, 1967.
LÉVI-STRAUSS, C., *L'Origine des manières de table*, Paris, 1968.
LÉVI-STRAUSS, C., *L'Homme nu*, Paris, 1971.
MACKSEY, R. and DONATO, E., eds, *The Structuralist Controversy*, Baltimore, 1972.
PIAGET, J., *Structuralism*, London, 1971.
*SCHIWY, G., *Der französische Strukturalismus*, Hamburg, 1967.
*SIMONIS, Y., *Claude Lévi-Strauss ou la passion de l'inceste*, Paris, 1968.

4. Typology (see chapter 4)

AUERBACH, E., *Typologische Motive in der Mittelalterlichen Literatur*, Krefeld, 1953.
CHARITY, A. C., *Events and Afterlife, The Dialectics of Christian Typology in The Bible and Dante*, Cambridge, 1967.
DANIÉLOU, J., *Sacramentum Futuri*, Paris, 1950.
DANIÉLOU, J., 'The Problem of Symbolism', *Thought*, 25, 1950.
DANIÉLOU, J., *From Shadow to Reality*, London, 1960.
GOPPELT, L., *Typos*, Gütersloh, 1939.
*HANSON, R. P. C., *Allegory and Event*, London, 1959.
LAMPE, G. H. W. and WOOLLCOMBE, K. J., *Essays on Typology*, London, 1957.
LUBAC, H. DE, *Histoire et Esprit*, Paris, 1950.
RAHNER, H., *Griechische Mythen in christlicher Deutung*, Zürich, 1966.

5. The Transition from Mythic Imagery to Conceptual Thought (see chapter 6)

ALBRIGHT, W. F., *From the Stone Age to Christianity*, Anchor Books, 1957.
BEVAN, E., *Symbolism and Belief*, London, 1938.
BIDEZ, J., *Eos, ou Platon et l'Orient*, Bruxelles, 1945.
BUFFIÈRE, F., *Les Mythes d'Homère et la pensée grecque*, Paris, 1956.
COOMARASWAMY, A., *Hinduism and Buddhism*, New York, 1943.
CORNFORD, F. M., *From Religion to Philosophy*, Cambridge, 1912 and Harper Torchbooks, 1947.
CORNFORD, F. M., *Principium Sapientiae*, Cambridge, 1952.
DANCKERT, W., *Goethe, der mythische Urgrund seiner Weltschau*, Berlin, 1951.
*DOUGLAS, M., *Natural Symbols*, London, 1970.
FRUTIGER, P., *Les Mythes de Platon*, Paris, 1930.

GILSON, E., *The Christian Philosophy of St Thomas Aquinas*, London, 1957.
GILSON, E., *The Spirit of Medieval Philosophy*, London, 1936.
HAVELOCK, E. A., *Preface to Plato*, Oxford, 1963.
KERENYI, K., *Romandichtung und Mythologie*, Zürich, 1945.
LEVY, G. R., *The Gate of Horn*, London, 1948.
MUNZ, P., *Relationship and Solitude: A Study of the Relationship between Ethics, Metaphysics and Mythology*, London, 1964.
MURTY, K. S., *Revelation and Reason in Advaita Vedanta*, New York, 1959.
*SCHUHL, P. M., *Essai sur la formation de la pensée grecque*, Paris, 1949.
SNELL, B., *The Discovery of the Mind*, English trans., Cambridge, Mass., 1953 and New York (Harper Torchbook), 1960.
STEWART, J. A., *The Myths of Plato*, G. R. Levy, ed., London, 1961.
TRESMONTANT, C., *Étude de métaphysique biblique*, Paris, 1955.
TRESMONTANT, C., *Essai sur la pensée hébraïque*, Paris, 1956.
TRESMONTANT, C., *La Métaphysique du Christianisme et la naissance de la philosophie chrétienne*, Paris, 1961.
TRESMONTANT, C., *La Métaphysique du Christianisme et la crise du XIIIme siècle*, Paris, 1964.
WALCOT, P., *Hesiod and the East*, Cardiff, 1966.
WEST, M. L., *Early Greek Philosophy and the Orient*, Oxford, 1971.
YATES, F. A., *Giordano Bruno and the Hermetic Tradition*, New York, 1969.
ZAEHNER, R. C., *At Sundry Times*, London, 1958.
ZIMMER, H., *Kunstform und Yoga*, Berlin, 1926.
ZIMMER, H., *Myths and Symbols of Indian Art and Civilisation*, Washington, 1946.

6. Relationship between Myth and History (see chapters 6 and 12)

BARTSCH, H. W., ed., *Kerygma and Myth*, London, Vol. 1, 1954; Vol. 2, 1961.
*BAYET, J., *Histoire politique et psychologique de la religion romaine*, Paris, 1957.
*BURROWS, MILLAR, 'Ancient Israel', in R. C. Denton, ed., *The Idea of History in the Ancient Near East*, New Haven, 1955.
CORNFORD, F. M., *Thucydides Mythistoricus*, London, 1907.
DUMÉZIL, G., *Mythe et épopée*, Paris, 1968.
FINLEY, M. I., 'Myth, Memory and History', *History and Theory*, 4, 1964/5.
FRANKFORT, H. and H. A. *et al.*, *Before Philosophy*, Harmondsworth (Pelican Books), 1949; first published as *The Intellectual Adventure of Ancient Man*, Chicago, 1946.
FRISCH, M., *Wilhelm Tell für die Schule*, Frankfurt, 1970.
*GRANT, M., *Roman Myths*, London, 1971.
MACQUARRIE, J., *The Scope of Demythologising*, London, 1960.
MALEVEZ, L., *The Christian Message and Myth*, London, 1958.
MOMIGLIANO, A., 'An Interim Report on the Origins of Rome', *Journal of Roman Studies*, 1963.
MUNZ, P., 'History and Myth', *Philosophical Quarterly*, 6, 1956.
MUNZ, P., 'History and Religion', *Church Quarterly Review*, 157, 1956.
MUNZ, P., 'The Purity of Historical Method', *New Zealand Journal of History*, 5, 1971.
OESTERLEY, W. O. E., 'Early Hebrew Festival Rituals', in S. H. Hooke, ed., *Myth and Ritual*, Oxford, 1933.
THARPAR, R., 'La tradizione storiografica nell' India Antica', *Rivista storica italiana*, 80, 1968.

WIDENGREN, G., 'Myth and History in Israelite–Jewish Thought', in S. Diamond, ed., *Culture in History*, New York, 1960.

7. The Reduction of Myth to Non-Myth (see chapter 9)

ALLEGRO, J. M. *The Sacred Mushroom and the Cross*, London, 1970.
BASCOM, W., 'The Myth-Ritual Theory', *Journal of American Folklore*, 78, 1965.
FONTENROSE, J., *The Ritual Theory of Myth*, Berkeley, 1971.
GRAVES, R., *Adam's Rib*, New York, 1958.
GRAVES, R. and PODRO, J., *The Nazarene Gospel Restored*, London, 1953.
HYMAN, S. E., *The Tangled Bank*, New York, 1962.
KLUCKHOHN, C., 'Myths and Rituals', *Harvard Theological Review*, 35, 1942.
KUHN, A., *Physical Religion*, New York, 1891.
MOWINCKEL, S., *Religion und Kultus*, Göttingen, 1953.
MÜLLER, M., *Comparative Mythology*, A. Smythe Palmer, ed., London, 1909.
MUNZ, P., 'The Problem of "die soziologische Verortung des Gnostizismus"', *Numen*, 19, 1972.
PREUSS, K. T., *Der religiöse Gehalt der Mythen*, Tübingen, 1933.
RAGLAN, LORD, *The Hero*, London, 1936.
TURBAYNE, C. M., *The Myth of Metaphor*, New Haven, 1962.
SWANSON, G. E., *Religion and Regime*, Ann Arbor, 1967.
TOPITSCH, E., *Vom Ursprung und Ende der Metaphysik*, Wien, 1958.

8. Symbols, Images and Metaphors (see chapter 8, 11 and 12)

*ANDERSON, C. C., 'The Psychology of Metaphor', *Journal of Genetic Psychology*, 105, 1964.
BACHELARD, G., *La poétique de l'espace*, Paris, 1957.
BAENSCH, O., 'Kunst und Gefühl', *Logos*, Vol. 12, 1923; English trans., 'Feeling and Form' in S. K. Langer, ed., *Reflections on Art*, Baltimore, 1959.
BARTLETT, F. C., 'The Function of Images', *Brit J. Psych.*, XI, 1920–1.
BARTLETT, F. C., 'Feeling, Imaging, Thinking', *Brit. J. Psych.*, XVI, 1925–6.
BLACK, M., *Models and Metaphors*, Ithaca, 1962.
BLUMENBERG, H., *Paradigmen zu einer Metaphorologie*, Bonn, 1960.
BODKIN, M., *Archetypal Patterns in Poetry*, London, 1934.
BROOKE-ROSE, C., *A Grammar of Metaphor*, London, 1958.
CASSIRER, E., *The Philosophy of Symbolic Forms*, English trans., New Haven, 1953.
CHADWICK, C., *Symbolism*, London, 1971.
CHIARI, J., *Realism and Imagination*, London, 1960.
CORNELL, K., *The Symbolist Movement*, New Haven, 1950.
CROME, P., *Symbol und Unzulänglichkeit der Sprache*, Munich, 1970.
DIECKMANN, L., 'Friedrich Schlegel and Romantic Concepts of the Symbol', *Germanic Review*, 1959.
DIEL, P., *Le Symbolisme dans la mythologie grecque*, Paris.
DILLISTONE, F. W., ed., *Myth and Symbol*, London, 1966.
DORER, M., *Historische Grundlagen der Psychoanalyse*, Leipzig, 1932.
DURAND, G., *L'Imagination symbolique*, Paris, 1964.
ELIADE, M., *Images et Symboles*, Paris, 1952.
ELIOT, T. S., 'Hamlet and His Problems', in T. S. Eliot, *The Sacred Wood*, London, 1920.

FINK, E., 'Vergegenwärtigung und Bild', *Jahrb. f. Phil. und phänomenologische Forschung*, 11, 1930.
*FOWLIE, W., *Mallarmé*, Chicago, 1953.
FRYE, N., *Anatomy of Criticism*, Princeton, 1957.
FRYE, N., 'The Motive for Metaphor', in N. Frye, *The Educated Imagination*, Bloomington, 1964.
GOMBRICH, E. H., *Symbolic Images*, London, 1972.
HAWKES, T., *Metaphor*, London, 1972.
KAHN, G., *Les Origines du symbolisme*, Messein, 1936.
LANGER, S. K., *Philosophy in a New Key*, Cambridge, Mass., 1942.
LANGER, S. K., *Feeling and Form*, New York, 1953.
LAWLER, J. R., ed., *The Language of French Symbolism*, Princeton, 1969.
LEVIN, H., *Symbolism and Fiction*, Charlottesville, 1956.
PONGS, H., *Das Bild in der Dichtung*, 2nd ed., Marburg, 1960.
RAMSEY, I. T., *Models and Mystery*, London, 1964.
RAYAN, K., 'Rasa and the Objective Correlative', *British Journal of Aesthetics*, 5, 1965.
RAYMON, M., *De Baudelaire au surréalisme*, Corréa, 1933.
READ, H., *Education Through Art*, London, 1943.
READ, H., *The Forms of Things Unknown*, London, 1960.
SCHLESINGER, M., *Geschichte des Symbols*, Berlin, 1912.
*SHIBLE, W. A., *Metaphor*, Whitewater, 1971.
SPITZ, H. J., *Die Metaphorik des geistigen Schriftsinns*, München, 1971.
Symbol and Symbolism, Yale French Studies, 9, 1951.
SYMONS, A., *The Symbolist Movement in Literature*, London, 1899.
TINDALL, W. Y., *The Literary Symbol*, Bloomington, 1955.
VORFRIEDE, W., 'Die Entstehung des Symbols in der Dichtung', *Deutsche Rundschau*, 88, 1962.
WERNER, H., 'Die Ursprünge der Metaphor', *Arbeiten zur Entwicklungspsychologie*, Leipzig, 3, 1919.
WHEELWRIGHT, P. E., *Metaphor and Reality*, Bloomington, 1962.
WHITEHEAD, A. N., *Symbolism*, Cambridge, 1928.
YEATS, W. B., 'The Symbolism of Poetry', *Essays*, London, 1924.

9. The Theory of Mind and Feeling-States (see Chapters 8 and 11)

BOLLNOW, O. F., *Das Wesen der Stimmungen*, Frankfurt, 1943.
FINDLAY, J. N., 'The Logic of Bewusstseinslagen', *Philosophical Quarterly*, 5, 1955.
FINDLAY, J. N., *The Discipline of the Cave*, London, 1966.
FINDLAY, J. N., *The Transcendence of the Cave*, London, 1967.
*HILLMAN, J., *Emotions*, London, 1960.
HUMPHREY, G., *Thinking*, London, 1951.
KRUEGER, F., 'Das Wesen der Gefühle', *Archiv f. die gesamte Psychologie*, 65, 1928.
LAVELLE, L., *De l'Intimité spirituelle*, Paris, 1955.
MERLEAU-PONTY, M., *Phenomenology of Perception*, English trans., London, 1962.
MERLEAU-PONTY, M., *The Structure of Behaviour*, English trans., London, 1965.
MURDOCH, I., 'Nostalgia for the Particular', *Proceedings of the Aristotelian Society*, 52, 1951–2.
MURDOCH, I., 'Thinking and Language', *ibid.*, Suppl., 25, 1951.
PIAGET, J., *Biology and Knowledge*, Edinburgh, 1972.

*PLUTCHIK, R., *Emotions*, New York, 1968.
SMYTHIES, J. R., *Brain and Mind*, London, 1965.
*SMYTHIES, J. R., ed., *Beyond Reductionism*, London, 1969.
TITCHENER, E. B., *Experimental Psychology of the Thought Processes*, New York, 1909.
WERNER, H. and KAPLAN, B., *Symbol Formation*, New York, 1963.

10. Abstraction in Art (see chapter 8)

*EHRENZWEIG, A., *The Hidden Order of Art*, London, 1967.
*GILSON, E., *Painting and Reality*, Meridian, 1959.
*GRASSI, E., *Kunst und Mythos*, Hamburg, 1957.
KAUFMANN, F., 'Art and Religion', *Philosophy and Phenomenological Research*, I, 1940.
READ, H., *Art and Alienation*, New York, 1969.
ROSENBERG, H., *The Anxious Object*, London, 1965.
SEDLMAYR, H., *Die Revolution der modernen Kunst*, Hamburg, 1956.
WIND, E., *Art and Anarchy*, London, 1963.
WORRINGER, W., *Abstraction and Empathy*, English trans., London, 1953.

11. The Problem of Theological and Metaphysical Knowledge (see chapters 7 and 11)

BAMBROUGH, R. B., *Reason, Truth and God*, London, 1969.
BOWLES, P., *Is Metaphysics Possible?* London, 1965.
BRAITHWAITE, R. B., *An Empiricist's View of the Nature of Religion*, Cambridge, 1955.
EMMET, D., *The Nature of Metaphysical Thinking*, London, 1949.
FARRER, A., *The Glass of Vision*, London, 1948.
FLEW, A. G. N., ed., *New Essays in Philosophical Theology*, London, 1955.
HEIMSOETH, H., *Die sechs grossen Themen der abendländischen Metaphysik*, Stuttgart, 1958.
HOOK, S., ed., *Religious Experience and Truth*, London, 1962.
LAZEROWITZ, M., *The Structure of Metaphysics*, New York, 1955.
MACINTYRE, A., ed., *Metaphysical Beliefs*, London, 1957.
MARTIN, C. B., *Religious Belief*, Ithaca, 1959.
MASCALL, E. L., *Words and Images*, London, 1957.
MAVRODES, G. I., *Belief in God*, New York, 1970.
MUNZ, P., *Problems of Religious Knowledge*, London, 1959.
RAMSEY, I. T., ed., *Prospects for Metaphysics*, London, 1961.
WATKINS, J. W. N., 'The Haunted Universe', *Listener*, 21 and 28 November, 1957.
WOOD, R. E., ed., *The Future of Metaphysics*, Chicago, 1970.

12. Symbols and Depth-Psychology (see chapter 10)

BASTIDE, R., *The Sociology of Mental Disorder*, English trans., London, 1972.
BENEDICT, R., 'Anthropology and the Abnormal', *Journal of General Psychology*, 10, 1934.
BERES, D., 'Symbol and Object', *Bulletin of the Menninger Clinic*, 29, 1965.
BINSWANGER, L., *Grundformen und Erkenntnis menschlichen Daseins*, 4th ed., München, 1964.
BURROW, TRIGANT, *The Structure of Insanity*, London, 1932.

COOPER, D., *Psychiatry and Anti-Psychiatry*, London, 1967.

FLEW, A., *Crime or Disease?*, London, 1973.

FOUCAULT, M., *Madness and Civilisation*, English trans., London, 1965.

GUNTRIP, H., *Personality Structure*, New York, 1961.

HOLT, R. R., 'The Development of the Primary Process', in R. R. Holt, ed., *Motives and Thought*, New York, 1967.

JONES, E., 'Theory of Symbolism', in E. Jones, *Papers on Psychoanalysis*, 2nd ed., London, 1918.

KUBIE, L. S., *Neurotic Distortion of the Creative Process*, Lawrence, 1958.

LAING, R. D., *The Divided Self*, London, 1960.

LORENZER, A., *Kritik des psychoanalytischen Symbolbegriffs*, Frankfurt, 1970.

MAY, R., ed., *Existence*, New York, 1959.

MILNER, M., 'The Role of Illusion in Symbol Formation', in M. Klein *et al.* eds., *New Directions in Psychoanalysis*, London, 1955.

MINKOWSKI, E., *Le Temps vécu*, Paris, 1933.

MINKOWSKI, E., *La Schizophrénie*, Paris, 1953.

RICOEUR, P., *Freud*, New Haven, 1970.

RODRIGUÉ, E. 'Notes on Symbolism', *International Journal of Psychoanalysis*, 37, 1956.

ROYCE, JOSEPH, R., *Psychology and the Symbol; an Interdisciplinary Symposium*, New York, 1965.

RYCROFT, C., 'Symbolism in its Relation to the Primary and Secondary Processes', *International Journal of Psychoanalysis*, 37, 1956.

RYCROFT, C. *Imagination and Reality*, London, 1968.

SEGAL, H., 'Notes on Symbol Formation', *International Journal of Psychoanalysis*, 38, 1958.

SCHULTZ, J. H., *Grundfragen der Neurosenlehre*, München, n.d.

SEGEL, N. P., ed., 'The Psychoanalytic Theory of the Symbolic Process', *Journal of the American Psychoanalytical Association*, 9, 1961.

SZASZ, T. S., *The Myth of Mental Illness*, New York, 1961.

SZASZ, T. S., *The Manufacture of Madness*, London, 1971.

WHITE, V., *God and the Unconscious*, London, 1952.

WINNICOTT, D. W., *Playing and Reality*, London, 1971.

INDEX

139

DATE DUE